CW01019504

METAPHOR
IN
AMERICAN SIGN
LANGUAGE

METAPHOR
IN
AMERICAN SIGN
LANGUAGE

Phyllis Perrin Wilcox

Gallaudet University Press

WASHINGTON, D.C.

Gallaudet University Press
Washington, DC 20002

The entire section on GIVE-*concede* in chapter 6 was first published in
The Linguistics of Giving, ed. J. Newman (Amsterdam: John Benjamins, 1998) and
is printed here with permission from John Benjamins Publishing Company.

Library of Congress Cataloging-in-Publication Data

Wilcox, Phyllis Perrin.
    Metaphor in American Sign Language / Phyllis Perrin Wilcox.
    p. cm.
    Includes bibliographical references and index.
    ISBN 1-56368-099-8 (hardcover : alk. paper)
    1. American Sign Language. 2. Metaphor. I. Title.

HV2474.W545 2000
419—dc21
                                                            00-047654

Sign illustrations by Kip Toddington Fletcher

For Kay Triplett Adams McIntyre—who said "Let's meet halfway" so many times when we were younger and lived a block from each other in Ponchatoula, Louisiana. You taught me that good things can happen when a person believes in herself. The many hours, days, and years that I sat reading while waiting for you to get off work at the town library led to my deep interest in words. For your inner strength and your honesty and the security that you provided in my life, Kay, this book is dedicated to you.

Contents

Illustrations

Acknowledgments

Several years ago, an undergraduate sign language interpreting major at the University of New Mexico (UNM) approached me and asked that I direct her to "a book on metaphors in American Sign Language." Our search turned up no such book. During the subsequent years I became interested in the experiential theory of metaphor that linguists of spoken languages were exploring. When I enrolled in anthropologist Keith Basso's graduate class at UNM, he introduced me to the metaphors that Apache Indians use on the reservations in Arizona. During this class he also assigned his students to read a small book called *Metaphors We Live By* (Chicago: University of Chicago Press, 1980). The groundbreaking mappings that authors Lakoff and Johnson define in that book for spoken languages led me to a steadfast fascination in signed language metaphors. This book is the product of that interest and the result of studies to determine how American Sign Language (ASL) uses metaphors to talk about language and thought.

I would like to acknowledge John Benjamins Publishing Company for allowing graphics and substantial sections of "GIVE: Acts of Giving in American Sign Language," from *The Linguistics of Giving,* edited by John Newman (1998), to be reprinted in this book. The reader is referred to the Benjamins publication for the full article.

I am grateful to the students at the University of New Mexico who helped during various stages of the evolution of this book, especially Charlie Wilkinson, Susanne Lee, Michelle Coronado, and Jennifer Lizut.

Consultants who graciously extended their knowledge to the GIVE research were Leticia Arellano, Gabriel Arellano, Antoinette Eidson, Mickey Jones, J. M. Lee, Bob Moore, Henri Grau, Bonnie J.

Rudy, Sandra Sandoval, Cleo Torrez, Gloria Delgado Wickham, Amy Wickham, and Amy Willman. Consultants for research on metaphorical mapping were Patsy Bennett, Simon Carmel, Perry Connolly, Patrick Graybill, Leslie Greer, Dan Lucero, Robert Otero, Fernando Savon, Della Stiger, and Luke Walker. International consultants were Simon Attia, Jean-Yves Augros, Patrick Belossine, Henri Bimont, Benno Carramore, Jerome Caillon, Veronica Gillot, Carole Guttian, Claudia Jauch, Chantal Liennel, Soya Mori, and Christian Rathmann. I am especially indebted to Marie-Louise Fournier. I appreciate the contributions of the deaf scholars from France, Switzerland, Italy, and the United States who added their input during my workshops and lectures on metaphor and metonymy. Special gratitude goes to my "French connections": Alex Bonucci, Paula Bramante, Courtney "Coco" McKee, and Delphine Massicard. I am grateful to Betsy McDonald (Rochester, New York), Penny Boyes-Braem and Patty Shores Hermann (Zurich, Switzerland), and Elena Pizzuto (Rome, Italy) for helping to arrange the sessions with consultants.

In addition, I benefited from, and enjoyed, discussions about metaphors with Keith Basso, M.J. Bienvenu, Patrick Boudreault, William Croft, Terry Janzen, Judy Kegl, George Lakoff, Barbara O'Dea, Jo Santiago, Joanne Scheibman, Ted Supalla, and Barbara Shaffer. Theoretical guidance and support came from Joan Bybee, Larry Gorbet, Vera John-Steiner, Betsy McDonald, Gladys Levis-Pilz, Eve Sweetser, and Sherman Wilcox. Any misconceptions or errors are entirely my own.

Time and again Ivey Pittle Wallace from the Gallaudet University Press encouraged me to continue writing; I appreciate her support and confidence.

This book would not be the same without Keith Cagle's contribution. A native user of ASL, whose brother is also deaf, he is the son of deaf parents. Not only did he honor my work by being the language model for this book, but I am indebted to him for demonstrating through his actions what it means to be a true deaf professional.

ACKNOWLEDGMENTS

Special appreciation belongs to my husband, Sherman, my beloved partner and friend. I could not have completed this book without his constant assistance and encouragement every page of the way.

Typographical Treatments

The conventions used by other linguists for identifying metaphors and similes have been modified in this text to accommodate the inclusion of American Sign Language glosses, metaphors, and similes. The following treatments have been applied:

ASL glosses: small capital letters (GIVE)

English metaphors: bold lowercase letters (**the mind is a container**)

English similes: bold, italic lowercase letters (***she runs like a gazelle***)

ASL metaphors   bold small capital letters (**IDEAS IN EXISTENCE ARE STRAIGHT**)

ASL similes   italic small capital letters (*INDEX LIKE TRAIN*)

What mysteries are embedded in a sign?
The simplest words in ASL have passed through
the hands of thousands of deaf people. The
motions have been repeated millions of times.
What happens to the shape and to the meaning of
common signs in ASL when they have been
breathed on and embodied daily by deaf people?
What metaphors have mapped onto the knuckles,
fingers, skin, and bones of a sign?

Introduction

Night threw a cloak of diamonds over the lake. Educated speakers of English will recognize the previous sentence as containing a metaphor. Some people may not understand what constitutes a metaphor, but they accept without much thought that a colorful line of prose can be metaphorical.

In the past, metaphors were considered to be mysterious and poetic. Until recently, a metaphor was considered to be just a flowery bit of prose. People who studied metaphors once thought that they violated grammatical rules, therefore, they were considered to be deviant linguistic structures. Metaphors did not represent literal reality. Thus, metaphors were falsehoods that only added misleading little frills to the real purpose of our language.

Metaphors have been set apart from the literal domain of language since Aristotle's time. This exclusion was partly based on the pervasive hold that the classical theory of categorization had on philosophical thinkers and educators through the ages. People sought the "truth," and metaphors were thought to lead them away from that goal.

Because the issue of what constitutes a metaphor deals substantially with the comparison of categories, it is important to have a clear idea of what constitutes a category. Traditional theories of metaphor are based on the so-called classical set, which has as its criterion a membership of equality. A more recent theory of categorization is called prototype theory (Rosch 1973; Rosch and Lloyd 1978). The difference between these two theories is central to an understanding of experiential metaphorical meaning. According to the classical theory, membership in a certain category is determined by shared properties or characteristics. For example, to belong to

1

the "category of birds," a creature must have feathers and a beak and must be able to fly. Anything that does not have those characteristics is simply not a bird. A category is considered to be fixed, uniform, and permanent; objects belong to a category according to a fixed definition of the set. In this classical viewpoint, reasoning is abstract and objective.

Traditionally, the classical objectivists view meaning as a rule-governed objective correspondence between abstract symbols in sentences and their counterparts in the literal world. Objects possess inherent properties that can be identified according to the classical sets in which they belong. These sets are thought to be inflexible categories based on shared properties that are independent of humans and their particular understanding of the sets. By this reasoning, metaphors are considered an intentional misuse of language because the classical theory presumes an absolute truth in the world. Traditional metaphors (figures of speech) are not experienced and are, therefore, literally false.

In other words, objectivist meaning is based upon the "truth" of a statement. The classical categorical objectivist viewpoint on meaning includes the following views:

1. Categories, even biological sets, are defined by common essential properties.
2. The mind is seen as separate and independent of the body, with emotions having little conceptual importance.
3. Grammar is considered a matter of pure form only.
4. Reason transcends human cognition; there is a single correct way of understanding what is and is not true, and all people are governed by the same conceptual assumptions. (Lakoff 1987b, 8–9)

The classical category has clear membership status, with every member equally sharing common properties or features or functions. But studies are now challenging the classical theory on categories. Instead of all members of a set being equally represented, with no one member having special status, Rosch (1973) proposes that membership is based on prototypes. In other words, there can be a "best example" in a category set. The most representative members of a set are known as the prototypical members, and they best represent that particular category. Zadeh (1965) accords categories with graduations of membership. For example, instead of all men being equally defined members of the set representing males, graduated categories of membership are used in order to indicate varying degrees of shortness or richness. Sweetser extends graduated membership to word meaning and says that meaning is frequently "prototype-based rather than being composed of checklists of features" (1990, 16–17), as required by classical category membership. Therefore, according to prototype theory, there can be "bad birds and better birds" (Aitchison 1987, 51–62).

Another argument challenging the objectivism of categories is "markedness," as used in linguistic analysis. This represents what Lakoff describes as "a kind of prototype effect—an asymmetry in a category, where one member or subcategory is taken to be somehow more basic than the other" (1987b, 60–61). Some morphological and phonological categories "mark" a feature. A cognitively simpler feature in a linguistic category, usually the shortest or most easily produced form, is referred to as the unmarked form (60–61). In American Sign Language (ASL), the unmarked handshapes are those learned first by deaf infants and children (McIntire 1977).

Johnson says that it is not possible to understand the speaker's logic "without understanding the basic, irreducible metaphorical structure that holds it together" (1987, 5). In Sweetser's work on diachronic and synchronic analysis of multiple meanings, she states, "Our linguistic system is inextricably interwoven with the rest of our physical and cognitive selves" (1990, 6). Johnson's and Sweetser's arguments are in opposition to a semantic theory that eliminates cognitive organization from our linguistic system.

The past century has seen a shift in the way people look at the classification of thought itself and has brought about a change in how we perceive and how we categorize things in our world. The recognition that we use metaphors pervasively when we think is revolutionizing how linguists look at metaphors. A growing body of philosophers, linguists, and educators are countering the traditional concept of metaphor theory. People are now examining metaphorical mapping in order to understand the process of human thought.

At the same time the mappings of metaphor and other tropes were being studied by linguists of spoken languages, the study of metaphors in ASL was confounded by a phenomenon that prevented an accurate analysis. Looking at the moving hands of a signer while trying to separate the handshapes and the movements into metaphors only created a smoke screen of confusion. Metaphorical mapping in ASL was obscured by the issue of iconicity, or the fact that some signs bear a close physical resemblance to the object they represent. The problem then became how to define a metaphor in ASL. Other questions soon arose: When a native user of ASL produces a sign, how does the phonological form of that grammatical gesture relate to metaphorical extensions? Is there a semantic change with a subsequent change in movement? Does metaphorical extension affect the form of a sign? How does the iconicity of a sign affect its meaning? What can the linguistic intuition of native signers tell us about metaphorical mapping in ASL? Lexical items produced within the semantic domains of language and thought by fluent users of ASL are analyzed and described in this book in an attempt to answer these questions.

There are opposing viewpoints among the various signed language linguists represented in this book. Nevertheless, the opposing viewpoints, especially those dealing with iconicity, have created the dynamic theories now being offered regarding how metaphors operate. The perspectives and insight that opposing scholars have brought to the study of metaphor theory show how the cognitive processes experienced by deaf people change and enrich signed languages.[1]

---

1. Throughout this book the term *deaf* refers to people who are hard of hearing or profoundly deaf, people born deaf into a cultural milieu (native users of ASL), and those who learn ASL postlingually. In some cases, reference will be made only to people who are considered to be culturally deaf; then the conventional use of a capital D (*Deaf* as opposed to generic *deaf*) will be used.

INTRODUCTION

In order to understand ASL metaphors, we have to understand the current theories on metaphor and related tropes. Traditionally, the cognitive force of a conventional metaphor comes from the reconceptualization of information that we already have. New perspectives on the metaphorical extension of cognitively structured concepts are currently being examined by cognitive linguists and others in different disciplines. This book extends the study of metaphor to signed languages and offers a stepping-stone for individuals who are interested in looking deeper into issues of metaphorical mapping in ASL.

The questions explored in this book originated from my initial inquiries into this topic: What is a metaphor? What defines metaphoric mapping and how is it constrained? Why is there so much variation among researchers regarding the identification of metaphorical referents? Are similar referential counterparts found in ASL? This book will not resolve all questions raised. However, it provides a basic corpus of metaphors used by native signers of ASL and provides evidence that signers use metaphors to talk about language and thought.

Chapter 1 provides background on metaphor theory. In order to analyze metaphors in ASL, one must have a basic concept of a metaphor. There are different theories to consider before settling on a specific hypothesis from which to structure research. A number of theories are presented, along with their respective metaphorical components, before introducing the model that is the basis of this study, the experiential theory of metaphor. Several categories of tropes are highlighted, with the main focus on experiential metaphors. Because we model our linguistic expressions on an understanding of social and physical environments, the impact that cultural values of a community have on metaphor will also be noted.

Chapter 2 offers information on classifiers and iconicity, because these linguistic features are relevant to the analysis in later chapters. Research on metaphors and metaphorical mapping in ASL is not extensive. In fact, the linguistic research in this area has begun only recently, often with contradictory results. Several relevant dissertation theses and studies will be discussed in order to compare analyses and findings.

Chapter 3 deals with the methodology and the design of the studies in this book, a description of the consultants and settings, and the procedural methods used. The ethnographic methodology is not the focus of the studies; rather it was used to obtain raw data for the linguistic analysis. This analysis was based on the experiential theory that our linguistic expressions are generated through physical and cognitive interdependency.

In chapter 4 experiential mapping of ASL is found in the interaction of metaphors, metonymy, and similes. The hypothesis that deaf people use metaphors in the language and thought domains is supported from the analysis of the research data. Supporting evidence is also obtained from various resources of ASL (dictionaries, textbooks, certified interpreters of ASL, and commercial videotapes). Chapter 5 analyzes metaphors and metonymy through expressions that represent basic spatialization, orientation, and ontological and structural metaphors. Chapter 6 extends metaphorical mapping from a synchronic investigation to a diachronic search on language change. The etymology of the ASL sign GIVE is tracked from its origin in *langue des signes française* (LSF) to modern ASL. Chapter 7 looks at the impact that culture can have on the comprehension of metaphors and metonyms. Individuals and groups from Albuquerque, New Mexico; Zurich, Switzerland; and Rome, Italy, provided input for that study.

1

WHAT IS A METAPHOR?

Scholars who study metaphor theory have not always agreed on what constitutes metaphor as a unit of discourse. Traditionally, metaphors were considered to be full sentences (Black 1962). More recently, metaphors have been identified in different grammatical components and can be contained in a word (Sweetser 1987b); a phrase (Kittay 1987); an entire poem, proverb, or literary passage (Lakoff and Turner 1989); or even at the morpho-phonemic feature level (Boyes-Braem 1981). A metaphor might even be only implied within the text (Kittay 1987).

The most consistent description found in both classical and experiential definitions of metaphors, however, is that a metaphor represents two domains of semantic fields. These two different semantic domains can be labeled and defined in various ways and have different meanings.

Richards (1936) was the first to coin terms for the two concepts that operate simultaneously in the formation of a metaphor: *tenor* and *vehicle*. He did not explicitly define these concepts, but Kittay later suggested that "the *vehicle* is the idea conveyed by the literal meaning of the words used metaphorically. The *tenor* is the idea conveyed by the vehicle" (1987, 16). However, context becomes essential when defining referents, as shown in the following sentence: **man is a wolf.** The metaphorically used "wolf" and the term *wolf* with its usual beastly connotation lend ambiguous readings to this one word. Kittay suggests that additional confusion is created if the *vehicle* is perceived as being equivalent to what was traditionally called the *image* (1987, 25). Images occur more frequently with traditional metaphors than with nonmetaphorical language.

Black calls the metaphorical unit (in his view, the sentence) the *frame,* and the word or words otherwise used metaphorically, the *focus* (1962, 39). Meaning is imposed on the focal word by the entire frame of the sentence. Kittay describes the frame as "that minimal unit which establishes the incongruity" (1987, 24). The frame might be as small as a phrase or greater than the passage that the focus word is in, or it may not even be a part of the contextualized language being addressed. The less explicit the frame, the more possibilities there are in determining the metaphorical interpretation.

Black originally referred to the *tenor* as *principal subject* and the *vehicle* as *subsidiary subject.* Kittay retains the use and definition of Black's *vehicle,* with its suggestion of transport, to denote the focal term in a metaphor (1987, 26). She refers to the *tenor,* however, as the *topic.* This topic suggests what the text is about and picks out what is named or spoken of in the metaphor. Thus, for metaphorical extension to take place, a transference of relations from the semantic field of the vehicle to the conceptual domain of the topic occurs.

Kittay also explains that there may exist "bridge" terms, which influence the interpretation of the correct application of the focal term (1987, 165–66). For example, if the field of the text provides a topic that is to convey a metaphorical use of the word *seal,* cognitive selection would eliminate the semantic connotation of *seal* as used to apply to important documents if bridge terms such as "clever tricks" or "waddling walk" were found within the frame of the metaphor. The mammal and its linguistic connotations would then be cognitively retrieved for the eventual juxtaposition of semantic references.

The field of the vehicle in a metaphor takes on the role of the originating field, according to Kittay. This provides for the asymmetrical analogies of metaphorical extension: "one side of the analogy has privileged status in regard to the other" (1987, 152). It is this originating (vehicle) source that produces and generates the relevant contrasts in the metaphor. However, only some, but not all, relations of contrast are mapped onto the semantic field of the topic of the metaphor.

Metaphors change language. According to Mac Cormac, metaphors operate as cognitive processes that produce new insights (1985, 2). Mac Cormac sees the creator of metaphor as retrieving and mapping long-term memory combinations of words that are not normally associated (1985, 129). The resulting similarities, as well as dissimilarities, then generate new meanings. Comprehension of these new meanings depends on whether the receiver involved can see the connection between the two concepts associated in this unusual juxtaposition.

People do not intentionally create false statements as a way to express concepts in ordinary language production. They do not present nonliteral statements with the devious intention of providing falsehoods when describing something. Metaphors, however untrue they may seem when examined literally, are intended to enlighten, not to deceive. Yet philosophers have long been concerned with the mercurial quality of metaphors and their ability to confuse the issue of truth. In fact, some theories of metaphor were created in part as an attempt to resolve this issue.

As an example, the controversion theory, developed by Beardsley (1976), allows for metaphors to collapse into analogies in order to prevent deviancy from the truth. Converting a metaphor to a simile through the use of the terms *like* or *as if* might reduce the element of falsehood, but it would also stifle the creative intent conveyed by the metaphor in the first place.

Kittay (1987) contends that metaphors do more than compare two concepts. A literal comparison, perhaps of schools and libraries, or of grapes and squash, may compare set categories of similar institutions or foods. A metaphor, however, crosses domains of categories. Metaphors create similarity by referring to concepts in different categorical boundaries—for example, comparing grapes and libraries. The different referents of a metaphor, coming from two distinct categories, exert a tension that generates a new meaning (183). Metaphors help us to assimilate information already within our conceptual organization. Kittay says, "The cognitive force of metaphor comes, not from providing new information about the world, rather from a (re)conceptualization of information that is already available to us" (39).

Theorists in the first half of the twentieth century who attempted to understand the cognitive framework of metaphor held various perspectives on the crossing of semantic domains and the transference found in metaphorical mappings. The experiential metaphor, as described later in this chapter, is the foundation for research in this book. Nevertheless, an understanding of the traditional components of metaphorical extension and how they function is important for the subsequent analysis of ASL metaphors.

Tropes

The study of metaphor will inevitably involve a discussion of tropes, which are categories of figures of speech. People studying tropes have placed the number of tropic categories to be anywhere from several to more than sixty. Linguists, researchers, anthropologists, philosophers, and educators studying tropes have recognized a variety of categories of tropes: Friedrich (1991) looks at the categories of metaphor, modal, and contiguity, each of which maintains subgroups of polytropic interaction; Crystal's (1987) *Encyclopedia of Language* cites metaphor and simile as the most widely recognized forms; Lévi-Strauss (1967) and Fernandez (1986) offer primacy to metaphor over metonymy; Quinn (1982) defines and documents over sixty tropes in his *Figures of Speech,* including antithesis, metonymy, syncope, and synecdoche, but not metaphor. There is controversy over which trope should be designated a "master" trope, with candidates other than metaphor being considered (Friedrich 1991; Ohnuki-Tierney 1991). I do not designate any of the commonly researched tropes as most important, but it is important to examine several tropes other than metaphor in order to better understand what constitutes a metaphor.

Traditionally, tropes have been studied in a compartmentalized manner, with each tropic category serving as a mutually exclusive model. For example, metaphor is often discussed as if it "consisted only of the figurative identification of the features of source and target overtly involved in the metaphoric comparison" (T. Turner 1991, 153). Goossens differentiates between metonymy (as well as synecdoche) and metaphor: "in a metaphoric mapping two discrete domains are involved, whereas in a metonymy the mapping occurs within a single domain" (1990, 325). Even though metaphor and metonymy are generally recognized as being distinct cognitive processes, Goossens coined a term for the interaction of metaphor and metonymy in expressions for linguistic action: *metaphtonymy* (323). He uses this term to generate awareness of the fact that metaphor and metonymy can be intertwined in countless linguistic situations. The fuzzy boundary lines between domains, as well as the nonlinguistic and linguistic action of a reading, can affect the interaction of tropes. For example, *to catch someone's ear* can have a literal meaning, as well as a metonymical mapping (an ear representing a whole person) to designate the process of getting someone to listen and pay attention (334–35).

Anthropologists and others besides Goossens have begun to consider the "fluid and complex nature of polytropes" (Ohnuki-Tierney 1991, 181) and to look at them from the perspective of interactive transformations on different levels. A diachronic (historical) as well as a synchronic (one point in time) analysis is crucial to the correct interpretation of a tropic expression. In fact, Kittay argues that whether we characterize a term as metaphorical or literal may depend on which analytical stance is taken (1987, 21). Goossens demonstrates that some domains, such as *sound,* "have a hybrid character, in that they are metonyms in some contexts, metaphors from metonymy in others and sometimes undecided between these two interpretations in actual contexts" (1990, 329). Terence Turner believes that figurative and literal meanings are not fixed but can be shaded and changed into one another depending on the context (1991, 129). Language use generates tropic change.

Although the most recent research indicates fluid diachronic and synchronic interrelationships between tropes, the following sections briefly categorize several tropes relevant to the focus of this book: simile, metonymy, synecdoche, and experiential metaphor. These three tropes other than metaphor demonstrate metaphorical extension against a background of tropic relationships. By contrasting these related tropes, we can more accurately identify metaphor in ASL.

Simile

Crystal (1987, 70) defines simile as two unlike things being explicitly compared in order to point out a similarity, while using a marker such as *like* or *as:*

> I wandered lonely   a cloud
> That floats on high o'er vales and hills.
>
> (William Wordsworth, "Daffodils")

Separating simile from metaphor is difficult. They both suggest similitude. Gibb and Wales admit that "in contrast with what is known about metaphoric structure, little light appears to have been shed on the structure of simile" (1990, 201). However, there is a greater sense of focus on similarity in simile than in metaphor.

Regardless of commonalities attributed to both simile and metaphor, they are not interchangeable. According to Gibb and Wales, both forms are found to be equally effective as forms of communication. In their 1990 study, however, affect (feeling) was influenced by the form of the expression selected. A strong preference for the metaphoric form in sentences coincided with a higher level of intensity rating.

These findings help to clarify the theoretical position of non-equivalence between the two forms. There is a functional difference between metaphor and simile, views of the controversion (comparison) theory notwithstanding. The controversion theory sees metaphor as nothing more than an implicit simile, with metaphorical statements being reducible to similes. However, Gibb and Wales point out systematic differences in conditions that determine preference for either expression (1990, 199–213).

Using figurative sentences of the form "A [noun] . . . a [adjective] B [noun]" in which the only factor manipulated was concreteness of either the tenor (A) or the vehicle (B), certain variables were found to be possible points of differentiation between the two forms (Gibb and Wales 1990, 203). One finding showed that similes seemed to be preferred in the case of concrete vehicles, whereas metaphors were chosen in the case of abstract vehicles. For example, in the statement "The ocean . . . a lapping giant," there is a concrete tenor (ocean) followed by a concrete vehicle (giant). Both nouns are of a concrete nature, where concrete is defined as "being easily visualized but also associated with particular instances of an event" (Paivio et al. 1968, cited in Gibb and Wales 1990, 204). When native English-speaking subjects were requested to insert *is* or *is like* in place of the ellipsis points to complete the comparison statement, this type of statement consistently generated preference for simile as opposed to metaphor.

When the tenor was preceded by a definite article or possessive pronoun, as in the statement above about the ocean, the specificity of the tenor did not differentiate between patterns of form preference. However, concreteness of adjectives preceding the vehicles contributed to a preference for the simile form over the metaphor, as in "Her mouth was like a watchtower bugle" (Gibb and Wales 1990, 204). Although concreteness in general was a predictor of preference for the simile form, overall it seemed that vehicular concreteness was the major determinant of the preference.

The tag *like* makes obvious an intention to convey a relationship, according to Gregory and Mergler (1990). In their experiment, the tag *like* provided an invitation to "search for similarities." The response time required to decide the truth of sentences in simile form, such as "A fruit is like an orange," was greater than for a true metaphor (170). Gregory and Mergler also found that participants tended to respond more often "yes, the sentence makes sense" to false sentences in the simile form than they did with the false metaphor form. Participants also tended to take a longer time to determine whether the simile forms were false. The researchers hypothesized that the participants seemed to make use of their own subjective associations when weighing the highly shared attributes of the two categories involved. This affected the time needed to consider the literal sense of the total content of the sentences.

In a study on domain interaction performed by Trick and Katz (1986), a similar finding showed higher comprehensibility when there is greater distance between domains. People tend to understand metaphors that compare terms from dissimilar domains (such as actors and aircraft) more easily than metaphors that compare similar or identical domains (such as oranges and tangerines).

Kittay says that simile and metaphor use some of the same cognitive processes to promote parallels and analogies but that simile does not have what she calls "second-order meaning," the double semantic content carried by metaphor through the content that frames the vehicle (1987, 143). However, the nature of comparison found in similes, in particular with the use of *like,* should be understood metaphorically. She believes that simile signals a cross-categorical comparison (as when a large mammal is compared to a powerful institution) that is capable of creating a similarity rather than simply recording an antecedent one (19).

Kittay's understanding of simile is closer to Lakoff and Turner's (1989) than to the grammar-school distinction that similes are simple figures of speech. Lakoff and Turner stress that attempts to define metaphor or simile in terms of syntactic form miss the concept of what metaphorical mapping involves. They say that both forms can employ conceptual metaphor. "The kind called a simile simply makes a weaker claim" (Lakoff and Turner 1989, 133). One concept is still being understood in terms of another, regardless of the grammatical form of the statement.

The relationship between metaphors and similarity is complex. Ortony notes that "even though it may be incorrect to claim, as some have, that metaphor is *merely* a statement of similarity, it is probably not incorrect to say that metaphor is *largely* a statement of similarity." He uses the following example to illuminate this point: "According to this view, that is why one can say 'Metaphorically speaking, jogging is like a religion,' but not 'Metaphorically speaking, a cult is like a religion'" (in Gregory 1987, 480).

Searle tells us that even with the acceptance of a simile theory, we do not know "how to compute the respects of similarity or which similarities are metaphorically intended by the speaker" (1986, 103). There is still much dispute regarding the distinction between simile and metaphor. The simile, while looking deceptively simple, nevertheless represents further challenges to researchers intent upon understanding the cognitive differences between simile and metaphor. This blurring of tropic categorization carries over into the analysis of ASL simile found in chapter 4.

Metonymy and Synecdoche

The *American Heritage Dictionary* (3d ed.) defines metonymy as "a figure of speech in which one word or phrase is substituted for another with which it is closely associated, as in the use of *Washington* for *the United States government*." At first reading, this definition appears to be simplistic. The example given provides us with an immediate understanding, and this may be due to our ability to automatically comprehend metonymy without conscious effort. Yet metonymic referents are complex and not easily isolated.

While metaphor has always been associated with creativity, metonymy and synecdoche have been traditionally seen as representing a lesser degree of creative thinking. This perception probably derives from the fact that metonymy and synecdoche involve "only relations within the same natural domain" (T. Turner 1991, 149). An example of this simpler relationship is found in the synecdoche "branch," which is a metonymic figure for "tree" (Kittay 1987, 291).

Yet Lakoff considers metonymy to be "one of the basic characteristics of cognition" (1987b, 77). Lakoff further suggests that a metonymic mapping (letting one thing stand for another for some purpose) occurs within a single conceptual domain that is structured by an idealized cognitive model (ICM).[1] These cognitively evoked models are grounded in everyday experience and are fundamental to our conception of the world. Fillmore (1982) offers an example of *bachelor* as a word whose meaning involves an idealized cognitive model: although Tarzan fits the definition of a bachelor by virtue of being an unmarried adult man, his life hardly qualifies

---

1. Lakoff acknowledges four sources in the development of this cognitive model: Fillmore's frame semantics (1982); Lakoff and Johnson's theory of metaphor and metonymy (1980); Langacker's cognitive grammar (1986); and Fauconnier's theory of mental spaces (1985).

as a perfect example of bachelorhood. Lakoff claims that being able to take two cognitive models, in this case, Tarzan and bachelor, and compare them, noting the ways in which they overlap and the ways in which they differ, is "irreducibly cognitive" (1987b, 71). In other words, "An idealized cognitive model may fit one's understanding of the world either perfectly, very well, pretty well, somewhat well, pretty badly, badly, or not at all" (70).

In Lakoff's experiential theory, metonymy assumes a large and rich position within the realm of cognitive processing. Metonymic models include: making quick judgments about people and situations (stereotypes); making inferences from typical to atypical cases, based on knowledge of the typical (typical cases); making judgments of quality and planning for the future (ideals); making comparisons and using them as a model for behavior (paragons); defining concepts by principles of extension (generators); estimating size, doing calculations and making approximations (submodels); and making judgments of probability (salient examples) (1987b, 367).

One such metonymic model elaborated on by Lakoff is the housewife-mother stereotype (1987b, 79–85). This subcategory of *mother* is used to stand for an entire category of nurturing mothers, thereby making it a potential prototypical metonymic model. This model can also be identified with the typical case model, in which a typical case (housewife) stands for the whole category (mothers) (86).

Lakoff and Turner find that metonymy is frequently confused with metaphor (1989, 103–4). However, there are differences. Metonymic concepts allow one concept to stand for another, as in "We need some new *blood* in the organization." Blood stands for new members with fresh ideas. The metonymic concept of a part standing for a whole allows us to systematically conceptualize one thing by means of its relation to another. Metonymy, like metaphor, can be conventionalized and is often used automatically without conscious awareness. But metonymy requires a kind of cognitive manipulation that is different from metaphorical use.

A traditionally recognized subtype of metonymy is *synecdoche*, in which a word that represents only part of a whole is used to represent some larger whole. In other words, one aspect of an object is highlighted, while others are excluded. For example, "Put your heads together on that problem" emphasizes the parts of the people involved that are being highlighted in the statement. The heads contain the brains, which are relevant to solving a problem. "Put your toes together" would not convey the mental activity involved in working together to solve a problem.

Personification occurs when an object is thought of in terms of a person. Lakoff and Turner recognize that this mental conceptualization occurs naturally and readily because as humans, we can best understand things that relate to ourselves (1989, 72). Abstract ideas become more readily understood when they are clothed with personification.

When President Clinton began wearing an inconspicuous hearing aid, the phrase "The White House is hard of hearing" showed metonymic mapping via (1) the place for the institution mapping where the White House represents the United States government and (2) personification, where the White House is understood in terms of a hard of hearing person who does not perceive sounds well. The sentence exhibits metaphorical mapping with the source domain of physically impaired ears mapping onto the target domain of the person or institution who is unable to readily comprehend public opinions.

Durham and Fernandez suggest that the metaphorical juxtaposition of a source domain and a target domain often works metonymically, as in the slogan "Put a tiger in your tank." They illustrate that the tiger in the fuel tank creates a new perception, with the wild animal becoming metonymically part of both the car and the driver. They recognize this "metonymically sensitive understanding of a metaphor" and claim that "practically every metaphor that works effectively to associate domains, therefore, carries metonymic implications" (1991, 193).

Ohnuki-Tierney also finds that the fundamental basis of cultural discourse and social performance consists of relatively complex, interactive tropic constructs. This is illustrated by the following definition of synecdoche: a polytrope that involves analogy between two semantic domains metonymically linked as a result of metaphorical predication. According to Ohnuki-Tierney, synecdoche must meet two conditions: (1) two distinct semantic categories become metonymically related, and (2) there is an "interpenetration" or embeddedness of metaphor and metonymy taking place simultaneously (1991, 187).

Synecdoche is then distinguished from metonymy, which is characterized by part-for-whole or contiguity (continuous) principles, by the involvement of two semantic categories. Synecdoche is, however, distinguished from metaphor by the formation of the metonymic relation between the two domains. Instead of being a totally distinctive principle, Ohnuki-Tierney claims that synecdoche is "a more complex form of trope" due to the involvement of both metaphoric and metonymic principles and thus "differentiates itself from an ordinary metonymy or metaphor" (1991, 187).

Ohnuki-Tierney notes what is called the "beguiling power of synecdoche," as in the use of the majority group representing all minorities—the Americans (1991, 179). One holistic image can stand for the literally hundreds of melting-pot minorities actually represented in the nation. In the whole-for-part or part-for-whole relationships characterized by synecdoche, it is also possible to broadly apply ideology or political allegory (for example, "the Russians," "the Skinheads").

Terence Turner says, "'Synecdoche' may be defined, in general terms, as a specific relationship between metaphor and metonymy, as when a part of a whole (a metonymic relation) also replicates the form of the whole (a metaphoric relation)" (1991, 148). Kittay also sees a difference between synecdoche and metonymy as exemplified in the expression "a blond" when used to speak of a person with blond hair. She notes that there is a synecdoche of part-for-whole, blond hair for the person, as well as the metonymic transfer of blond for blond hair (1987, 296). However, Turner notes some instances of synecdoche as a more dynamic resulting structure: "metaphor and metonymy, rather than functioning as primary and mutually autonomous tropic principles, emerge as relatively secondary, contextually specific, and internally related refractions of the more complex master trope, synecdoche" (1991, 151). In other words, the whole structure of relations between metaphoric and metonymic dimensions can be an instance of synecdoche.

Lakoff and Turner see tropic interactions between the conventional metonymy **name stands for reputation** and the conventional metaphor **good is white; bad is black** in the expression "Charcoal/writes everybody's name/black" (1989, 184–85). This proverb has the charcoal, which is inherently black throughout, mapping onto a person who is inherently bad. This tropic interaction yields the interpretation that the slanderer will indiscriminately slander others. Lakoff and Turner note that such interaction between the two tropes occurs frequently.

Croft understands metonymy as a continuum between clear-cut cases of part-for-whole examples and the highlighting of highly intrinsic facets of a concept, which he refers to as "domain highlighting" (1991, 6). This allows the appropriate selection of an element of meaning from any of the domains of encyclopedic knowledge that make up the entire semantic structure of a word. The element, or elaboration site, is used to heighten an aspect of meaning that is relevant to the predication of the appropriate concept. Croft determines that there is no sole basic meaning attributed to a word; all possible peripheral meanings are available for consideration. Metonymy allows the domain selection of one of the elements that will most clearly highlight the intrinsic facets of a concept. For example, "We need a couple of strong *faces* for our football team" highlights the selection of a weak metonymic (synecdoche) choice from the domain matrix available for conceptual consideration. Croft's view of metonym is broader and offers a more encyclopedic characterization of part-to-whole concept than was traditionally adopted for the study of metonymy.

In some instances metonymy is considered to be a major trope, in others, a subtype of synecdoche. In some cases, synecdoche is considered to be a subcategorization of metonymy. Once again, the tropic scholars are at odds when differentiating between tropes. The boundary lines between cognitive domains are fuzzy, which is why there is a lack of agreement about the distinctions between various tropes. The merging of domains underlies the interaction and interpenetration among the four tropes illustrated in this chapter.

Experiential Metaphor

I. A. Richards (1936, 108–9) initiated interest in metaphors in the twentieth century by claiming that linguistic metaphors are manifestations of underlying metaphoric thought processes. In 1936 he wrote, "We cannot get through three sentences of ordinary fluid discourse [without the use of metaphor]. We think increasingly by means of metaphors that we profess *not* to be relying on. The metaphors we are avoiding steer our thought as much as those we accept" (92).

Lakoff and Johnson state that "no metaphor can ever be comprehended or even adequately represented independently of its experiential basis" (1980, 19). They argue for a systematicity of metaphorical concepts that they demonstrate are represented in expressions used in everyday activities. Groups of culturally related people will typically talk about things in a systematic way. These systematically presented concepts are pervasive and define everyday cultural reality and physical relationships with the surrounding environment.

Lakoff and associates' arguments lay the foundation for the current exploration of metaphorical concepts in ASL. The metaphorical extensions we use every day are automatic and common. This observation contradicts the traditionalists' viewpoint of metaphor in figurative use, which was considered to be rarer, more ornate, and accessible more to literary masters than to the person on the street.

Metaphors are conceptual mappings, according to Lakoff and Turner (1989). A source image can be mapped onto a target image through the conceptual cognitive framework involving a three-part structure: two endpoints (the source and target schemas) and a bridge between them (the detailed mapping). Thus, a source domain concept can be used to express a corresponding target domain concept, as when the term *withered* is applied to both plants and to people (107).

Turner proposes, "In metaphoric mapping, for those components of the source and target domains determined to be involved
in the mapping, preserve the image-schematic structure of the target, and import as much image-schematic structure from the
source as is consistent with that preservation" (1990, 254). In other
words, slots in the source domain get mapped onto slots in the target domain successfully when the mapping is constrained and has a
good "fit." This echoes the Invariance Hypothesis that was first described by Lakoff and Turner in *More Than Cool Reason* (1989). In
the metaphor **life is a journey**, we understand the more abstract
notion of that long period that makes up a lifetime by mapping
concrete experiences that we have had taking a journey or a trip
someplace. The cognitive activation of the source domain (journey) being mapped upon the target domain (life) results in a culturally shared mental image of the inferential structure associated
with journeys. We map early-morning departures, side trips to a su-
permarket, layovers at an airport, detours on the highway, arriving
at a hotel late at night, and so forth. Trips we have physically taken
enable us to comprehend the much longer experience of a lifetime.
We mentally accept only the source domain mappings of a journey
that contribute to our understanding of the target domain of life.
Lakoff and Turner describe this conceptual functioning as "an ef-
fortless and virtually unconscious mapping of aspects" (1989, 131).
*****Life is a bottle of aspirin**[2] does not have as many successful in-
stantiations of source domain mappings as does **life is a journey**—
unless a clever metaphor maker can successfully show how the bottle of aspirin we purchase at the pharmacy relates to the experience
of life itself. Not everything can be mapped successfully from one
domain to another. It is not the case that "anything can be anything" (Lakoff and Turner 1989, 203). We have to have experiences
in our culture and our everyday lives that allow us to readily accept
and understand the mappings.

---

2. The star conventionally represents an ungrammatical or unacceptable linguistic form.

Metaphorical mapping does not involve simply comparing two domains and noting similarities, however. Bidirectionality of the mapping does not occur. In English-speaking cultures, embarking on a trip is not thought of as "a birth," and arriving at a destination is not considered "a death." Nor do we automatically infer that as in life, we can experience only one journey. Our metaphorical language does not map both ways. However, two different metaphors might share two domains, differing in which is the source and which is the target; for example, **machines are people** and **people are machines.** Even in these metaphorical look-alikes, different references are mapped in a constrained way—with the will and desire of a person being attributed to machines, and the fact that machines idle or accelerate, break down, and need to be fixed being mapped onto the cognitive image of humans (Lakoff and Turner 1989, 132).

Bidirectionality is thus constrained and is created according to the cultural and social context of a body of people. Mapping takes place one way, from the source domain onto the target domain, with partial reference transferal only. In fact, this unidirectionality of mapping is a critical difference between metaphor and metonymy. There is a systematicity to this metaphorical highlighting and hiding, however. A subtle case of how a metaphorical concept can hide or highlight an aspect of our experience is exemplified through Reddy's "conduit metaphor" (Lakoff and Johnson 1980, 10). Reddy (1979) states that the English language is structured by the following complex metaphor:

Ideas or meanings are objects.
Linguistic expressions are containers.
Communication is sending.

The conduit metaphor allows a speaker to place ideas (as objects) into words (containers) in order to send them along (through a conduit) to another person who then presumably understands them without difficulty. Reddy (1979) has documented over a hundred types of expressions in English that he estimates account for more than 70 percent of the expressions used to talk about language. In the sentence "Your words seem hollow," the context is understood in terms of the part of the conduit metaphor that states that **linguistic expressions are containers.** The conduit metaphor is a conventional way to think about language. Lakoff and Johnson (1980) point out that Reddy's conduit metaphor requires that meanings have an existence independent of people and contexts. Supposedly, the ideas "sent" to another person can always be "opened up" and understood by any receiver. However, although Lakoff and Johnson concede that the conduit metaphor for communication does map knowledge about objects in containers onto an understanding of communication, they further believe that meaning is not necessarily explicit in contextual isolation. They offer the following as an example—"We need new alternative sources of energy"—to show that the president of Mobil Oil and the president of Friends of the Earth would probably have entirely different interpretations of this sentence (12). The meaning is not found within the words themselves but is determined by the social and political attitudes of the person who is conveying the sentence and the person who is listening.

Thus, a sentence may be ambiguous for contextual reasons, as in the sentence "My son sent the silent one." More explanation is needed in order for the receiver of this discourse to know that the "silent one" refers to a message (a card) the son decided to mail after some pondering over which card was most appropriate. In this instance, there was a phrase on the inside cover of the card in question that quoted a Native American Indian saying: "Hear the whisper on the wind." Not only was the message referring to the calmness of a desert breeze, but the colors on the card were soft pastels, inspiring thoughts of quiet, subdued beauty. An alternative card displayed bright, bold colors and catchy jingles. Which one did the son send? The conduit metaphor would be unable to convey an accurate meaning of the term "silent one" unless all discourse participants knew the content of the conversational environment (two cards were being considered).

In other words, the conduit metaphor will not apply to cases "where context is required to determine whether the sentence has any meaning at all and, if so, what meaning it has" (Lakoff and Johnson 1980, 12). In addition, the above example is complicated by a *physical* object being sent—the card. Therefore, the metaphorical object, the linguistic message itself, was obscured further by a literal, physical item overlapping with the conduit reference. Although metaphors can extend the range of understanding that people have during discourse, they can also constrain concepts so that they may be extended in some ways but not others.

In addition to its ability to highlight or hide aspects of the domain understood, the conduit metaphor also serves to categorize and motivate contextually induced properties relating to the communication of thoughts, ideas, and linguistic expressions. It is a rich, pervasive folk model found in many languages to create linguistic expressions dealing with the transferal of a speaker's thoughts along a conduit to a receiver's mind.

Lakoff and Johnson have identified several other basic kinds of metaphors that support their hypothesis that metaphorical concepts are experientially grounded. One is the *orientational* metaphor, which organizes a whole system of concepts with respect to one another (1980, 14). Most of these metaphors have to do with spatial orientation such as up-down, in-out, front-back, deep-shallow, and central-peripheral. These metaphors appear in our linguistic repertoire due to our physical and cultural experiences. There is nothing arbitrary about the fundamental organization of spatialization metaphors. They are rooted in the experiential basis of our everyday lives. Lakoff and Johnson argue that there is an "internal systematicity to each spatialization metaphor" (17). Their meanings do not represent random, isolated occurrences in discourse.

An example of an orientational metaphor, **happy is up**, is part of a coherent system rather than an isolated and random case of linguistic expression (Lakoff and Johnson 1980, 14–21). The ability to overcome a natural phenomenon such as gravity is considered to be positive. Expressing a concept using the word *up* typically conveys positive, happy feelings and concepts. *Up* is visualized as an increase or an upward movement in many typical daily occurrences. Water is added to a glass, and we see the greater volume as the water level rises. Blades of grass, exemplifying life, grow upward. All things being equal, physical height psychologically correlates with strength, power, and health. An upward spatialization usually indicates greater physical substance.

It is important, nevertheless, to realize that verticality can give rise to many different kinds of experiential metaphors. Prioritization often takes place when considering metaphorical and cultural coherence. Lakoff and Johnson show how the orientational **more is up** has priority over the **good is up** metaphor (1980, 23). Assuming that inflation and crime are "bad" and therefore should be spatialized downward, metaphorical expressions such as "Inflation is rising" and "The crime rate is going up" show the priority of **more is up** over **good is up.** Lakoff and Johnson base this prioritization on the physical experiential prominence of our lives, which is deeply entrenched in our culture and our language. Not all the values held by the members of our culture are equal, which may lead to different associations with the metaphors associated with those values. The complexity of orientational metaphors is extended in chapter 5 through the analysis of ASL.

Ontological metaphors allow an experience to be viewed as an entity (Lakoff and Johnson 1980, 26). "Events and actions are conceptualized metaphorically as objects, activities as substances, states as containers" (30). Examples include referring ("We are working toward *peace*"); quantifying ("There is *so much hatred* in the world"); identifying aspects ("His *emotional health* has deteriorated recently"); identifying causes ("He did it out of *anger*"); and setting goals and motivating actions ("He went to New York to *seek fame and fortune*") (26–27).

In American culture a powerful ontological metaphor, **the mind is an entity,** specifies that the mind is an object that can be held, broken, snapped, and even operated as a machine (Lakoff and Johnson 1980, 25–29). The mind is seen as an object because people are physical beings, experiencing the world as objects themselves. Set off in containers of skin, humans experience a separateness, an in-out orientation. While the orientational metaphor allows a simple in-out conceptualization to occur, the ontological metaphor allows more elaborate spatialization concepts in more specific terms. People move from room to room or from location to location. It is easy to extend this experience of territorial boundaries to the brain and further map onto the mind the concept of a container, with ideas entering and exiting.

In fact, it is so easy to structure thoughts in this way, that most persons are scarcely aware of a closely related supportive metaphor that Lakoff and Johnson consider fundamental to the human capacity to think, the *container* metaphor (1980, 29–30). This metaphor is so pervasive and natural that most people use this mental phenomenon as an integral model of the mind without being aware that they do so (for example, "I can't hold all this information," "One more thought and my mind will explode"). Langacker conceives of this metaphor as the "concept of a discrete container, whose rigid sides define a sharp boundary between an inside and an outside" (1991, 508). He sees this basic metaphor as also being mutually supportive of, and coherent with, Reddy's conduit metaphor.[3]

Metaphors that allow richer metaphorical elaboration than either orientational or ontological metaphors are *structural* metaphors. These involve structuring "one kind of thing or experience in terms of another kind, but the same natural dimensions of experience are used in both" (Lakoff and Johnson 1980, 178). For example, structural metaphors allow the use of one highly structured concept, such as a journey, to structure another complex concept, such as life. In addition to using simple container or spatialization metaphors, we can ground our social institutions and linguistic behaviors in our experiential environment. The structural

---

3. However, Langacker advises that adoption of this prevalent folk model for research purposes could lead to erroneous theoretical conclusions: "The components of a complex expression should not be thought of as providing the material used to construct it—their function is rather to categorize and motivate facets of the composite structure, which often displays emergent or contextually induced properties that no individual component is capable of evoking" (1991, 508).

metaphor **time is a resource** is grounded in our concept of experience with time as a "substance" to be saved, measured, used wisely, and so forth (Lakoff and Johnson 1999, 161–69).

Structural metaphors can be rooted in more elaborate concepts than mere containers or directionality (Lakoff and Johnson 1980, 61–68). Abstract concepts can be understood through a multiplicity of possible concrete source domains. For example, *time* can be understood metaphorically and talked about as though it were a physical substance that can be quantified precisely and assigned values per unit according to the notions of a given culture. Structural metaphors allow more complex linguistic highlighting and hiding of what is collectively experienced than orientational or ontological metaphors. They allow whole conceptual systems from a source domain to be mapped onto equally rich conceptual systems of the target domain.

The metaphor **understanding is grasping** is rich and systematic but certainly not novel. *Comprehend* comes from Latin and once meant both "hold tightly" and "understand." The metaphor of grasping is now dead in *comprehend* but is still alive when grasp is used to mean *understand* (Lakoff and Johnson 1999, 125). The source domain of physical space and the target domain of thought lead us to understand *understanding* as a kind of physical grasping of mental objects, as expressed in the sentence "Cheri can't quite grasp the idea of autosegmentals." Many conventional metaphors remain powerful tools for communicating concepts in our daily language. A metaphor that is no longer "novel" does not necessarily go off to "die" a slow death from lack of use.

Dead metaphors are metaphors that have become so conventionalized that their metaphorical impact is almost negligible. Lakoff (1987b) believes that the term *dead metaphor* is a holdover from when everyday language was considered to be literal and metaphors were believed to be rare and inessential figures of speech. In other words, a dead metaphor was considered to be "a linguistic expression that had once been novel and poetic, but had since become part of mundane conventional language, the cemetery of creative thought" (143).

Lakoff and Johnson acknowledge that there are actual dead metaphors that have become part of the language (1999, 124). They explain that the word *pedigree,* which evolved from the image of a grouse's foot mapped onto a family-tree diagram, no longer offers linguistic mapping from that source domain. We no longer use the Old French term *ped de gris* to mean a grouse's foot in English. The source image is gone; the source terminology is gone. There can be no image mapping or terminology mapping. *Pedigree* is a dead metaphor. Yet conventionalized (non-novel) metaphors, as demonstrated with **understanding is grasping**, can lead to powerful and linguistically productive everyday language use.

When source domains are mapped onto target domains in metaphorical mappings, the mapping is not arbitrary. The constraints have to do with the forms of our experiences, and how those forms structure thoughts. Following Johnson (1987), Mark Turner uses the technical term *image-schema* for skeletal forms that structure our images of thoughts:

> We experience images in various modalities: a visual image of a road, an auditory image of a scream, a kinesthetic image of a pinch, an olfactory image of the smell of pine, and so on. No rich image is wholly unique; rather, it shares skeletal structure with other, related images. We have a skeletal image of a scream that inheres within our rich images of particular screams. . . . We have a skeletal image of a flat bounded planar space that inheres within our rich images of individual tables, individual floors, individual plateaus. We have a skeletal image of verticality that inheres within our rich images of individual trees, individual buildings, individual people. (1991, 57)

Image-schemas are skeletal images that are used in cognitive operations, such as in the conceptualization of a rising motion, or a dip, or a projecting arrow. They are very general structures, such as bounded regions, paths, centers, etc. Not only do humans conceive of visual images as structured by image-schemas, but concepts of time, of events in time, and of causal relations seem to be structured by image-schemas as well. In metaphorical mappings, there are constraints on relations between image-schemas. The Invariance Hypothesis mentioned earlier preserves the image-schematic structure of the target, and imports as much image-schematic structure from the source as is consistent with that preservation (Lakoff 1990; Turner 1990).

Conceptual metaphors map complex conceptual structures in a source domain onto conceptual structures in a target domain. Lakoff (1987b, 219) shows that they exist in the form of structural metaphors (**life is a journey, time is money**). On the other hand, an image metaphor maps a mental image of the source onto the target in a "one-shot" picture that is neither conventionalized nor used in everyday reasoning. The internal structure of the image is mapped, rather than the abstract propositional structure of a concept.

Johnson contrasts an image of a face against the image-schema of a face, demonstrating clearly that "image schemata are not rich, concrete images or mental pictures" (1987, 23). He states, "You can easily form an image of a human face that is full of detail—it can have eyes that are wide open, with one pupil larger than another; lips cracked from exposure to the sun; ears that stick out unusually far; a scar running beneath the left eye; a mole just to the right and below the left corner of the mouth; and on and on through one detail after another" (24). In contrast, the image-schema for a face has only a few basic features—lines for eyes and nose, and perhaps a circle for the head.

Lakoff and Turner offer a vivid example of an image metaphor in English: "My wife . . . whose waist is an hourglass" (1989, 90). The hourglass maps onto the woman's waist, with the middle of the hourglass corresponding mentally with the waist of the woman. No words prompt this correspondence. We perform conceptual mapping between conventional mental images with the part-whole structure of one image mapping onto aspects of the part-whole structure of another. Thus, image mappings "lead us to map conventional knowledge about the source-domain image onto the target domain in ways that extend but do not disturb what we know of the target domain" (92).

Semantically autonomous concepts are grounded in the habitual and routinely physical and social patterns of daily experiences. "The source domain of a metaphor is characterized in terms of concepts (or aspects of concepts) that are semantically autonomous" (Lakoff and Turner 1989, 113). They explain that we understand death as night by drawing on a conventional understanding that nighttime includes dark, cold, foreboding, and often, mysterious experiences. Our sensory apparatus has provided us with culturally commonplace experiences of nighttime that we can draw from when thinking about death in terms of night. Metaphorical mappings are grounded upon the patterns of experiences that we routinely live. Sweetser explains, "We generally use the language of the external world to apply to the internal mental world, which is metaphorically structured as parallel to that external world" (1990, 50).

Lakoff sees the experiential approach to cognitive thinking as a broad approach:

> Experience is instead construed in the broad sense: the totality of human experience and everything that plays a role in it—the nature of our bodies, our genetically inherited capacities, our modes of physical functioning in the world, our social organization, etc. Experientialism claims that conceptual structure is meaningful because it is *embodied*, that is, it rises from, and is tied to, our preconceptual bodily experiences." (1987b, 266–67)

Sweetser also has progressive ideas regarding metaphors and has sought to dispel "two fundamental misconceptions, (1) the idea that semantic change is whimsical and random in direction, and (2) the idea that metaphor is a 'frill' on the fabric of linguistic meaning, rather than a structural part of our meaning-system" (1987b, 446). She believes that one of the clearest ways to examine the regular direction of semantic changes is to note the tendency for words to change from a more concrete to a more abstract meaning via metaphor. This linguistic process is exemplified by Svorou's argument that spatial location expressions such as *in*, *in front of*, and *outside* "evolve in specific ways following predictable paths, going from the concrete and specific to the abstract and general in both semantic and morphological domains" (1986, 516).

Sweetser has presented a metaphorical model of thought and speech through a comparison of historical directions and metaphorical mappings in these two communication domains. She explores "metaphorical relationships which allow verbs referring to mental states (or reasoning processes) and speech exchange to develop historically from words that once signified physical motion or location" (1987b, 446). Along with Traugott (1985), Sweetser notes that speech-act verbs and mental-state verbs both often start as physical motion/location verbs. However, verbs describing speech acts do not develop mental-state senses. In other words, "I see" can mean "I know" but not "I say," because "cognition but not speech-exchange is metaphorically understood as physical sense-perception and most primarily as vision" (Sweetser 1987b, 448).

Sweetser (1990) draws data for her diachronic research of the current English vocabularies of mental states and speech acts from metaphors in the Indo-European language family. Many of the illustrated historical semantic shifts involved took place in Latin, before the words were borrowed into English. These metaphorical structures can be used to point out both the differences and the similarities between our views of speech and of mental states. For example, mental activity is seen as the manipulation of ideas (mental objects) inside or outside a mental space (as in, *He wrestled with that idea for a week*). Further, they may be placed in linear order or participate in a linear reasoning sequence, or they may be building blocks in a theoretical construct (e.g., *He lined up his ducks in a row*). Speech exchange, however, is normally metaphorically viewed as an exchange of objects (e.g., *We traded thoughts on the subject*). Therefore, verbs of speech are taken specifically from expressions indicating a mutual object-exchange process, while verbs of thinking are taken from other kinds of object manipulation, such as holding, setting in order, or grasping (Sweetser 1990, 18–22).

This chapter has provided an overview of several theories of metaphor. From the classical to the recent experiential theories, all attempt to define what constitutes and motivates a metaphor. While any theory of metaphor can offer enlightenment of this linguistic phenomenon, Lakoff, by his own admission, has turned the world of metaphor upside down: "the claim that metaphors are to be accounted for by a mapping from one conceptual domain to another results in a radical meaning change. *Metaphor* no longer means what it did before" (1986, 224).

I plan to extend the exploration of metaphor theory further by examining a language that is different in modality from the English language analyzed by Lakoff and colleagues. American Sign Language is not a spoken language. The mode of the language—visual/gestural—is inherently different from the auditory/vocal modality of spoken English. This difference has an impact on the metaphorical mapping of ASL, as well as an influence on the experiential theory of metaphor.

Cultural Impact on Metaphors

An additional complexity of metaphorical mapping comes from culturally constrained semantic patterns. References that are cognitively shared between humans are often determined by cultural and sociolinguistic principles. Metaphorical mapping cannot be understood without taking into account the impact of culture. Basso's work with the Western Apache led him to show that language properties are too often studied in an isolated vacuum: "Wrenched from their natural context like so many fish out of water and hung up for sale, the sentence types prized by transformationalists are arrayed and analyzed as if they had no place of origin, no relationship to the affairs of men, no purpose but to be dissected and, once laid open, awarded to the cleverest bidder" (1976, 115).

Basso researched metaphors of a type called "wise words," which were created by adult tribal members who had reputations for intellectual acumen and extensive cultural knowledge. This class of metaphors violated traditional semantic rules: the subjects' designative features are incompatible with the designated features of the predicates. Examples of what Basso called "appropriately ill-formed utterances" are "Lightning is a boy" and "Ravens are widows" (1976, 116). Through ethnographic study, Basso discovered that the "wise words" metaphors are regarded to be expressions of mild negative personal criticism; however, highly oblique socioeducational values were accomplished through their use.

These Western Apache metaphorical concepts were not accessible through mere comprehension of the vocabulary items in their disguised simile frames. Interpretation of the metaphors had to be attained through one's own individual "acts of discovery and recognition that reveal the existence of relationships where previously none were perceived" (1976, 110). If one looked at only the literal meanings of the words and their syntactic orderings but neglected the cultural norms and attitudes of the speakers that influenced the use of the language, one might overlook the need to accomplish certain objectives in the course of social interaction. For example, a "white man's" interpretation of typical "wise words" metaphors might be based on the visual similarities between the two referents. But the Western Apache adult derives interpretation from similarity in the actions, in other words, what the two referents *do* the same.

Basso states that through metaphor, "language and culture come together and display their fundamental inseparability" (1976, 117). Thus, metaphor functions to "augment the lexical semantic resources of linguistic systems, and serves as an indispensable device for adapting these systems to the changing communicative needs of their speakers" (1976, 117).

Kittay (1987) says that language does not focus on truth or falsity; instead it deals with an expressive form of pragmatic and cultural concepts. Language changes according to the language community's shifting conceptual framework. This continuous evolution is due to the community's alterations and perceptions of its surrounding cultural and physical environment. Metaphor, then, can be transient, shifting from displaced meanings to new uses.

The study of metaphor in ASL is concerned not only with isolated signs or words. Because we model our linguistic expressions on an understanding of social and physical environments, applicable cultural values of the Deaf community must also be considered. ASL is a natural language indigenous to the Deaf community in the United States and parts of Canada. The Deaf community's concept of itself has shifted through the years, and the metaphors used to describe this cultural group of people have also changed. Many of the earlier descriptions that deaf people chose to use when describing themselves included the term *silent*. There were "silent clubs" and "silent newsletters." The Deaf World Games was once called the International Silent Games. But currently there is a push to exclude what has become a weaker concept—silence—and to include terms having to do with "seeing," "vision," or "deaf" instead, as in Vision Day or Deaf Awareness Day. This effort stresses the positive aspects of the group, as determined by the Deaf community itself.

ASL is a language that makes use of vision to stimulate the development of lexical and grammatical phenomena. People who use ASL use their eyes for functional purposes beyond those of hearing people. Visual icons are incorporated into the discreteness of this visual language. Sight affects the people who depend upon it for linguistic and social purposes. Cultural bonds are created according to common experiences, and the visual dependency of this language is crucial in the bonding that exists among ASL users. People who use ASL become aware of visual and gestural mores and taboos that differ from those found in everyday spoken language experience. It is only natural to suspect that a language modality can stimulate change in linguistic behaviors as well.

Because deafness is a physical state, it should be easy to define. Objectively, a simple decibel measurement could determine who is deaf and who is not. But there is acknowledged ambiguity in that area due to the lack of standardization in the training of, and equipment used by, audiologists. Cultural implications further complicate the definition of deafness. A person with only a slight hearing loss of 40 decibels may consider himself to be culturally Deaf if (a) he was born of Deaf parents who use ASL primarily, (b) his native language is ASL, and (c) he embraces the values of the Deaf culture. On the other hand, a woman with a profound hearing loss, unable to understand speech even with a hearing aid, may consider herself to be hard of hearing if she does not embrace the use of ASL or the values of Deaf culture. There is no such thing as a rigid category of "deaf people" with a set definition for inclusion. To say, "I am Deaf" is more than a simple statement about one's hearing status. To label oneself as Deaf is to make a profound cultural declaration.

A metaphor is not simply a linguistic expression, a word or a sentence with a colorful flourish. It is a cognitive process of human understanding. We use metaphors to make sense of the experiences going on around us. We project from the physical domain of forceful interactions with objects that we see or hear or experience onto the domain of abstract thought. Many of the connections that we make across domains are experiential projections at the preconceptual level of our understanding. Thus we come to understand cultural and linguistic abstractions by way of preconceptual structures that are meaningful in a physical way. These conceptual patterns are not individual innate conceptions; they are culturally influenced by the interaction of the people surrounding us.

2

REMOVING THE SHROUD
OF ICONICITY

The iconic, mimetic aspect of American Sign Language (ASL) has always been apparent. During the first half of the twentieth century, its close association with isomorphic physical representations and actions gave it a questionable linguistic status. Offering a historical perspective, Stokoe notes that "before there was sign language research, when speech and language, and sometimes even thinking itself, were believed to be inseparable, no one could conceive of signing as language. Such a belief prevented sign language research from happening at all" (1990, 6).

The push in the late 1970s was for recognition of ASL as a language in the eyes of the hearing community. In order to achieve legitimacy, ASL had to meet the same criterion for arbitrariness that spoken languages exhibit—the relationship between a meaningful element in language and its denotation must be independent of any physical resemblance between the two. Gesturing and pantomime were considered to be a substantial part of "sign language." This created a long-standing confusion between iconicity and metaphoricity. The important components of a metaphor had to be identified, yet the iconic nature of ASL prevented a clear analysis of this essential trope. Borrowing McDonald's words, the "spectre of iconicity" (1982, vi) had to be attacked and scrutinized in order to determine the basis and motivation of metaphor and its extensions.

In the late 1960s and early 1970s new research began to change the social and political status of ASL. Linguists discovered that seemingly ordinary gestures could be governed by linguistic principles. Stokoe's classic works (1976, 1978) initiated a rush of important contributions toward linguistic research in ASL. Researchers at the Salk Institute for Biological Studies showed evidence of diminished iconic properties of ASL (Klima and Bellugi 1979). Signed languages were found to be as abstract as other languages in which linguistic symbols are essentially arbitrary—that is, the linguistic form bears little resemblance to the form of its referent. Thus, the iconic properties of the language were obscured.

Lending weight to the argument for arbitrariness was Frishberg's description of historical change in ASL (1976). She showed that there is a tendency for signs to become more opaque and less iconic over time. Signs that might have originally developed at the outer limits of the signing space eventually became constrained within the centralized region. Lower signs either rose to the center or became two-handed to counterbalance the limited ability of the eyes to take in signed information produced in the viewer's peripheral vision. Signs near the face that were originally two-handed often dropped the nondominant hand in order to avoid redundancy or unnecessary visual noise. The physical constraints of the eyes and body seemed to encourage diminished iconicity. In general, Frishberg's diachronic examination of signs showed that over time they tend to shift away from their imitative origins as pantomimic or iconic gestures and move toward more arbitrary forms (Klima and Bellugi 1979, 70).

Nevertheless, Salk researchers recognized that iconicity was an element at all levels of their language research. They saw a separation of ASL into "two faces of signs: the iconic face and the encoded, arbitrary face" (Klima and Bellugi 1979, 4). Looking at the arbitrary face, Klima and Bellugi claimed that "regular grammatical processes operate on ASL signs without reference to any iconic properties of the signs themselves; rather, they operate blindly on the form of signs. One of the most striking effects of regular morphological operations on signs is the distortions of their form so that iconic aspects of the signs are overridden and submerged" (1979, 30).

Looking at ASL's iconic face, however, led Klima and Bellugi to conclude that:

The iconic face does not show at all in the processing of signs in immediate memory. Historical change diminishes the iconic properties of ASL signs; some signs become more opaque over time, some completely arbitrary. Grammatical operations that signs undergo can further submerge iconicity. Thus many signs, while having their roots deeply embedded in mimetic representation, have lost their original transparency as they have been constrained more tightly by the linguistic system. (1979, 34)

Yet iconicity continued to pervade their research, and they found this linguistic phenomenon in newly coined signs that were frequently based on mimetic representation of shape, action, or movement. In the poetic expressions of signers, also, the iconic properties of established lexical items were exploited to add depth and artistic color.

McDonald's research on "handle" classifiers treated iconicity as a governing variable in the phonology and morphology of ASL (1982, vi). The rigid, arbitrary constraints applying to verb stem predicate classifiers could not preclude similarities between a sign's form in the lexicon and its real world counterpart. McDonald argued that even frozen signs that were no longer "transparent" in their derivations (such as "wash hair," which uses a classifier that resembles a bar of soap rather than liquids) are recognized through iconicity that is constrained morphologically (1982, 12). She states,

The goals of a classification of ASL iconic devices are very similar to those of standard linguistic analysis—to predict existing forms and their distribution, and to screen out non-occurring or non-allowed forms. In fact, we have contentions that standard linguistic analysis *cannot* accomplish its goal with regard to these data in ASL and that recourse to a "taxonomy of iconicity" or a "visual analogue system" is absolutely necessary for the explanation and elegant description of forms in ASL. (14)

Friedman said that "the iconicity and iconic phonological and grammatical mechanisms in ASL and in other sign languages are highly conventionalized. Iconicity, at least in Sign Language, does not in any way indicate lack of conventionality" (1977, 52). She felt that the visual/gestural modality "avails itself to every possible visual cue in its formation" and that it is because of this "high sense of visual stimuli that language in the visual mode tends to enhance its structure in ways that oral language cannot" (1977, 54). In the early years of research on ASL no one could ignore the iconic interplay, whether at the lexical, syntactic, or semantic level.

Until recently, there were conflicting opinions on what to expect from ASL in terms of iconicity. In the desire to recognize ASL as a "real" language, there were strong attempts to downplay suggestions of iconic expression. Many linguists, educators of deaf children, and teachers of ASL gave token recognition to iconicity at the lexical level, then rapidly shied away from the issue, thus avoiding the older controversy as to whether ASL should be considered a real language or simply picturelike mimetic gestures. There was a strong need to distance ASL from this latter perception in order to acquire the status of its linguistic equals.

On the other hand, a language executed in a spatial-visual coding medium can take advantage of available iconic opportunities unavailable to spoken languages. Liddell (1990) arrived at this realization while studying syntactic versus topological space in ASL. He points out that a referent can be equated with an ordinal tip locus (thumb or fingertips) when the agreement verb is directed toward that exact locus. Yet there is compelling evidence to show that a spatial image of the referent is sometimes necessary in order to be able to produce grammatical verb agreement. That is, a signer must conceptualize the location of an imagined body when constructing grammatical behavior of agreement verbs. One striking example is found in the sentence, "I asked the falcon on my forearm" (see fig. 1). In this example, a falcon rests upon the arm of its trainer at locus z. The agreement verb (ASK) directs reference to the bird, which has acquired a conceptualized body. The sign ASK is directed toward the head of the bird, since the result would be ungrammatical if ASK were directed toward the bird's claws (Liddell 1990).

Iconicity in Spoken Languages

Spoken languages, too, are motivated by iconic principles (Armstrong 1983; Bybee 1985; Fauconnier 1985; Fleischman 1989; Givón

REMOVING THE SHROUD OF ICONICITY

Figure 1. "I asked the falcon on my forearm."

Source: Reprinted with permission of the publisher from S. Liddell, "Four Functions of a Locus," in C. Lucas, ed., *Sign Language Research: Theoretical Issues*, (Washington, D.C.: Gallaudet University Press, 1990), 188. © 1990 by Gallaudet University.

1985, 1991; Talmy 1983). Bybee notes, "Linguistic expression is not entirely arbitrary, rather there is a strong correspondence between the content of a linguistic unit and the mode of expression it takes" (1985, 7). Iconicity is linguistically economical in terms of the processing time and mental effort involved. In fact, economy seems to be the primary motivation of iconic representation: "All other things being equal, a code experience is easier to *store, retrieve* and *communicate* if the code is maximally isomorphic to the experience" (Givón 1985, 189). Givón even goes so far as to say that "we ought to consider iconicity the truly general case in the coding, representation and communication of experience, and symbols a mere extreme case on the iconic scale" (1985, 214).

Iconicity is clearly found throughout spoken languages. In a survey of fifty distinct, unrelated languages, Bybee found that "relevance is reflected iconically in morphological expression" (1985, 12). Three ways in which this principle is revealed are: "(1) The more relevant a category is to the verb, the more likely it is to occur in a synthetic or bound construction with the verb; (2) The more relevant a morphological category is to the verb, the closer its marker will occur with respect to the verb stem; (3) The more relevant a morphological category is to the verb, the greater will be the morphophonological fusion of that category with the stem" (1985, 11–12).

Cross-linguistic documentation of conditional verbs contributes to our understanding of the extent and nature of iconicity. Especially graphic is the preliminary cognitive map on which
Traugott (1985, 300) diagrams "horizontal" iconicity involved in
the syntactic display of conditionals. It is not surprising that a perfunctory look at ASL conditionals finds the syntactic display to be
very similar to Traugott's rising pitch and accompanying fall (see
fig. 2).[1]

In ASL, raising the eyebrows, along with an upward tilt of the
chin and appropriate body incline, indicates the onset of the first
part of the conditional statement (Baker and Cokely 1980). The conditional is completed with a general downward fall of the eyebrows,
chin, and hands, following similar iconic movement paths of the in-
tonational patterns in the spoken language analyzed by Traugott.[2]

Lakoff and Turner claim that iconicity in language is "a
metaphorical image-mapping in which the structure of the meaning is understood in terms of the structure of the form of the language presenting the meaning" (1989, 156). Such mappings are possible because of the existence of image-schemas. For example, the
expected metaphorical stoppage of an if/then conditional clause
can map onto the expected pause of the lyrics in a poem, and the
resulting opposing force is perceived as being iconic. Lakoff and
Turner claim that iconicity can provide "an extra layer of
metaphorical structure" to a poem (1989, 157).

He comes, then I'll go.

Figure 2. Horizontal iconicity

1. I am grateful to Sherman Wilcox for pointing out this iconic horizontal
similarity of conditionals found between ASL and English.

2. The description of the conditional is for a citation form resulting in a general statement or a command. A more complex conditional that includes yes/no
questions or wh-questions may produce different body and eyebrow movements.

Langacker (1985) contributes further observations on iconicity by equating meaning with conceptualization. Even intangible, abstract notions like "subjectivity," which deals with complex perspectives of subject/object participant asymmetry, can be analyzed successfully from a functional, cognitive approach that recognizes iconicity. According to Langacker, "Our imagic capacity is the source of meaning and the necessary starting point for its characterization. It is no less crucial to grammar, for grammar is nothing other than the conventional structuring and symbolization of conceptual content" (1985, 147).

Iconicity in Signed Languages

Functional and cognitive linguists ascribe a deeply significant role to iconicity in spoken languages. Givón (1985, 1991) and Haiman (1985) suggest that linguistic form is often motivated by iconic principles. However, if an ASL metaphor is to stand alone on an analytical level, the important components of the metaphor must be identified and separated from iconicity. Only then can analysis clearly determine the basis and motivation for metaphor and its extensions. The following section details the work of linguists who have contributed to the discussion on metaphor and iconicity in ASL. Each of the linguists is responsible for paving a large section of the road that leads to a clearer understanding of metaphorical mapping in ASL.[3]

Mandel

Over twenty years ago, Mark Mandel (1977) and his colleagues Lynn Friedman and Asa DeMatteo studied iconicity and arbitrariness in ASL. Friedman predicted that "if we fail to consider the role of iconicity and insist on analyzing ASL with reference only to its arbitrary elements, we will fail to grasp the essential nature of its formational properties" (1977, 49–50). Mandel set out to establish a

3. Readers are referred to a forthcoming book on iconicity in ASL by Taub, *Language in the Body: Iconicity and Conceptual Metaphor in American Sign Language,* Cambridge University Press, and Liddell's (1998) "Grounded Blends, Gestures, and Conceptual Shifts" in *Cognitive Linguistics.*

framework of analysis based on iconicity and the form various elements take, which included in part the visual appearance of their referents. Mandel recognized that there are numerous iconic devices available in ASL and that their interrelationship is complex.

Mandel (1977) suggested that ASL uses a continuum of iconicity that ranges from close physical reproductions of a signed referent to gestures that have no apparent pictorial quality. He believed that arbitrariness does not exclude iconicity and felt that iconicity was especially significant with gestures that were metonymically iconic to the referents. For example, the sign THINK is iconic to a metonym of the referent when it is signed by touching the extended forefinger to the forehead, so that the forehead is a metonym for the brain and thoughts. Another example is OLD, articulated by pulling the fist down from the chin, as if stroking one's beard. Mandel called the object that was directly described by the gesture (i.e., the forehead/brain, the beard), the base of the sign (1977, 63).

Mandel did not describe THINK as being metaphorical. In fact, he avoided exploring the meaning of metaphor and appeared to equate it with metonymy. "It seems that the name 'metaphor,' were it to be used as a term in ASL linguistics, would be more aptly applied to a particular class of depiction, **substitutive depiction**" (1977, 65). Signs such as HOSPITAL, HOUSE, and TREE were included in this class (see fig. 3). "These images depended upon a metaphoric relation between the articulator and the base. The relation between fingers and the branches of TREE is of the same kind of relation we allude to in naming the 'head' and 'foot' of a dinner table, a page, or a street: namely metaphor" (65). Actually, the sign for TREE is an icon for a metonym. Mandel clearly saw the importance of iconicity in the analysis of ASL; however, he did not make a distinction between metaphoric and metonymic representations.

Boyes-Braem

In investigating the extent to which the theory of distinctive features developed for spoken languages could be applied to signed languages, Penny Boyes-Braem (1981) found a fundamental difference between the distinctive features of spoken languages and what

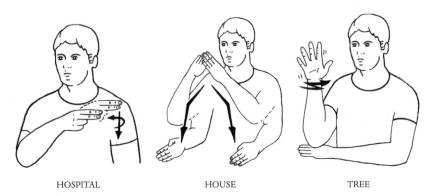

HOSPITAL   HOUSE   TREE

Figure 3. Substitutive depiction

she called "significant features" of ASL. Concerning the morpho-phonemic features of ASL, she found that there is often a connection between the components of the handshape and the meaning connected to the handshape. Spoken languages are seen to be free from "form–meaning bonds," thereby ensuring infinite number of possibilities for grammatical construction. Boyes-Braem's feature system captures patterns and regularities within ASL that allow the same degree of linguistic flexibility as spoken languages—the capacity to allow infinite internal linguistic relationships.

Boyes-Braem formulated her model of ASL lexical levels in 1981 (see table 1). Although she now acknowledges a misidentification in her description of iconicity and metaphor, Boyes-Braem's work presents "perhaps the most extensive discussion to date of visual metaphor in sign language" (Wilbur 1987, 171). The British linguist Mary Brennan agreed and called Boyes-Braem's work a "major contribution to the recognition of the role of metaphor within sign language lexical structure" (1990, 23). Her work so concisely provides an example of the difficulty of separating iconicity from metaphor that it will be discussed here.

While metaphors cross semantic boundaries and juxtapose two different domains or referents, iconicity refers to aspects of signs that are chosen on the basis of resemblance. Boyes-Braem looked at the signed words WRISTWATCH$_1$ (using the F classifier representing

Table 1. Boyes-Braem's Model of ASL Lexical Levels

Theory	Example
Level	
I. Underlying Concept Semantic Components	I. The concept of constructing an edifice or building
II. Symbolic Representation Level (the matching of the underlying concept or semantic components with a visual metaphor)	II. Visual metaphor of flat objects being piled on top of each other
III. Morpho-phonemic features selected to match the underlying visual metaphor (matching done directly or through an established ASL paradigm)	III. Flat objects represented by the handshape parameter specifically with the features: +linear, +surface, +/−full
IV. Underlying phonemic hands and possible variants resulting from feature selection	IV. (B)(H)
V. Final Surface Forms with allophonic variation	V. [B] [B] [H] [H]

Note. Adapted from Boyes-Braem (1981, p. 42).

the outline of the watch face) and WRISTWATCH$_2$ (using the Bent L classifier variant representing the strap circling the wrist). Both signs bear a high degree of physical resemblance to the real object, a wristwatch. Neither of these two signs represents separate semantic domains. The classifiers explicitly demonstrate a signed manifestation of a real object. Boyes-Braem originally claimed that this relationship was metaphorical. She now sees it as iconic.

At the "symbolic representation level" Boyes-Braem saw the underlying semantic concept as being matched up with "a visual symbolic representation or kind of visual *metaphor*" [italics added] (1981, 43). As an example of the underlying concept of constructing something, Boyes-Braem offered the visual metaphor in the ASL sign BUILD. "Obviously, the sign BUILD is not confined to referring to building walls; one uses the visual metaphor of a specific instance of building to carry the general semantic concept of constructing something" (43). While it is correct that BUILD can be categorized as a metaphor, the iconic movements of the hands cannot be labeled metaphorical based on their explicit iconicity. The movements and handshapes are iconic. The B and H classifier handshapes resemble the act of building as they are laid on top of each other. They are iconic movements for a prototypical act of building (i.e., laying of bricks and mortar, as opposed to hammering in nails). This is not metaphor.

Relationships, communications, trust, or any number of other abstract concepts can be "constructed" through the use of the BUILD sign. When BUILD is used this way, it becomes metaphorical, with two separate domains involved: (1) the source domain of physical construction and (2) the target domain of relationships or communicative systems or trust being "built up." It is not inclusion at the symbolic representation level that constitutes justification of metaphor status. It is the juxtaposition of two separate conceptual domains. In summary, we see that varied links are created. The articulation of BUILD is *iconic* as it shows the action of building a wall in a prototypical manner. This prototype is a *metonym* for the larger category that represents physical constructions of all kinds. The general act of construction is a source domain for the abstract target domain—the *metaphorical* building of a relationship.

Boyes-Braem's symbolic representation level, instead of constituting metaphoricity, appears to broach a framework for iconic representation in ASL: "Whereas the semantic elements in spoken language are usually related directly to patterns of morphological forms, in sign languages there seems to be an intervening symbolic representational level" (1981, 42).

In addition, Boyes-Braem's work on the diachronic phonological variants of ASL shows what combinatorial possibilities can be achieved through the morpho-phonemic representations of the perceptual forms of the language. However, she stated, "The visual metaphors set up at the symbolic representation level in ASL are almost always ones which allow the hands to *represent symbolically* the functions which they actually perform in daily life" (1981, 61).

Boyes-Braem now contends that the term *metaphor* employed in her work often referred to iconicity.

Gee and Kegl

James Gee and Judy Kegl (1982) proposed that the ASL verbal system supports the long-standing linguistic locative hypothesis that spatial expressions are more grammatically and semantically basic than various nonspatial expressions. The basic grammatical structures of many languages are founded on the notions of location and change of location. Gee and Kegl speculated that ASL's verbal system is also ultimately built up from such a locative base.

Gee and Kegl formulated a set of word formation rules, one of which was a process called *metaphorical extension*. Through this process the literal meaning associated with locative and inflectional verb stems is "extended to more abstract domains which form semantically extended verb classes such as emotion, perception or cognitive verbs" (Gee and Kegl 1982, 187). Basic verb classes are expanded to handle more abstract domains. The morphological one-on-one map (isomorphism) between ASL phonetic structure and its semantic structure allows this metaphorical extension to occur. Gee and Kegl illustrated this proposed metaphorical extension through the use of the G classifier. They proposed that the G classifier (long, thin object) represented *thought, sight,* and *sound.* There are "lines of thought, lines of sight, and lines of sound" that project outward from or inward to the body part associated with them (1982, 198). For example, they described the ASL sign THINK as "a line of thought" to be represented by an extended index finger located at the forehead.

In order to derive more abstract verbs of emotion, perception, and cognition, Gee and Kegl (1982) demonstrate that systematic metaphorical extension is expanded through the use of a rule called *theme incorporation.* This allows basic verb classes to handle more abstract domains through the expansion of the movement component of a simple or complex verb. They claim that this recursive rule allows for an infinite number of lexical items. In the case of the signs THINK and KNOW, the metaphorical extension derives from "the same vehicle classifier used to represent vehicles like cars, trucks or trains which is embedded into a [FROM#TO] verb whose leftmost location, the goal, is associated with the body part doing the perceiving" (1982, 196). In other words, the perceiver—the eyes, the ears, or the mind—is the contact location for the vehicle classifier that will "take in" the sight, sound, or thought from the environment. (While not subscribing to their use of a vehicle classifier to represent the sign THINK, my own analysis of the IDEAS IN EXISTENCE ARE STRAIGHT metaphor originated from Gee and Kegl's description; see chapter 5).

Gee and Kegl argue strongly that in the ASL verbal system "all or most grammatical and semantic structures in language ultimately derive from spatial notions" and that the spatial expressions derived are basic grammatical expressions that can be metaphorically extended to more abstract ones (1982, 185). This corresponds closely to Lakoff and colleagues' view that metaphorical extension derives from a basic experiential source domain to an abstract target domain.

Wilbur

Ronnie Wilbur (1987) established a small corpus of metaphors following the Lakoff and Johnson model (1980): spatialization metaphors, ontological metaphors, and structural metaphors. Her evidence of spatialization metaphors, paralleling orientational metaphors described by Lakoff and Johnson, was found by noting the direction of the movement of several signed words. For example, the metaphor HAPPY IS UP was demonstrated by signs with upward movements, such as CHEERFUL, HAPPY, and LAUGH (Wilbur 1987, 174). The NEGATIVE VALUE IS DOWN metaphor was instantiated by signs that move downwards, such as LOUSY, IGNORE, and FAIL. Wilbur noted that orientation of the palm was an acceptable physical indicator of up/down spatialization. In other words, it is not necessary for the up/down spatialization to be represented literally by an upward or downward movement.

Front-to-back spatialization is prominent in ASL. Wilbur documented a number of signs that move forward to represent the future, such as TOMORROW, NEXT-WEEK, NEXT-YEAR, and POSTPONE (1987, 175). Other signs move toward the back of the signer's body to indicate the past, including YESTERDAY, LAST-WEEK, LAST-YEAR, and RECENTLY. Signs also follow a forward movement from the back to the front to show continuity of time: HISTORY, GENERATION, SINCE (FROM-THEN-UNTIL-NOW). Wilbur finds this to be similar to perspectives on future and past that are found in English expressions, such as "I'm looking *forward* to next week's party" and "you can look *back* with pride at your accomplishments" (175).

Wilbur has also documented an ontological metaphor using an SASS (size-and-shape specifier) classifier handshape for "the mind is an expandable container" (1987, 177). The C classifier handshape is made at the forehead and can collapse or expand according to the general degree of knowledge metaphorically represented in the head/mind. Objects can be put into the container. Information can then be (metaphorically) placed in the container and handled through various classifier handshapes via the conduit metaphor (Reddy 1979). Wilbur explains, "People 'take' ideas (objects) from their minds (containers) and 'put' their ideas into words (containers) to transfer them to others so that they can get out the meaning (remove the ideas from the words and put them into their own minds)" (1987, 178–79).

In her 1987 work, Wilbur discussed what had been considered a group of apparently unrelated examples. The examples were taken from Frishberg and Gough's (1973) earlier work describing sign families, Boyes-Braem's (1981) symbolic representation level of visual metaphors, and Gee and Kegl's (1982) model dealing with metaphorical extension. Wilbur recognized that the cognitive framework provided by Lakoff and Johnson (1980) offered coherence to the analysis of these different models that was not previously apparent (1987, 173).

Most of the examples that Wilbur discussed were clearly metaphorical, as opposed to merely iconic. In addition, she noted that "finding structural metaphors in ASL is perhaps the hardest search" since internal patterns must be found, as opposed to the clearer correlations between spatialization and handshapes (1987, 179). Her analysis of BRILLIANT as being a structural metaphor is based upon an interpretation of the internal patterns of that sign. Using Lakoff and Johnson's framework, she looked beyond possible isomorphic handshape resemblance and identified the source domain as referring to a shiny concrete object and the target domain as being the intellectual "light" that represents understanding (i.e., UNDERSTANDING IS SEEING) (179–80).

While Wilbur did not explore metaphorical mapping in depth, her work provided another critical stepping-stone for others (this author included) who were exploring the newly emerging tropic phenomena.

Brennan

Mary Brennan, a linguist studying British Sign Language (BSL), wisely warned, "Anyone who attempts to explain or explore the notion of metaphor, either within language generally or within a specific language, does so, or at least, should do so with a considerable amount of trepidation. Here, indeed, we are treading on very dangerous ground" (1990, 19). Brennan recognized that there was still confusion regarding the iconic and metaphoric components of signed words.

Brennan proposed an account of word formation in BSL that suggests that "metaphorical relationships are an integral part of the structural organization of BSL and as such participate actively in the generation of new signs" (1990, 23). Brennan's corpus of data is extensive and represents an advancement in our understanding of productive morphology and word formation in BSL. She was certainly not swayed by the tendency on the part of some linguists to avoid the issue of iconicity:

It is interesting to note that this increasing interest in naturalness within mainstream linguistics comes at a time when, within sign linguistics, there is some hesitancy about giving too much weight to claims about the high degree of iconicity built into sign language systems. The claim inherent within this account of BSL morphology is that "iconic" elements provide a triggering role within the language. (184)

Brennan recognized that BSL has a pervasive metaphorical range and gives numerous examples of metaphorical expressions, but her description of metaphor still blurred the distinction between iconicity and metaphoricity. For example, Brennan says that real-world referents, whether concrete, abstract, or somewhere in between, are marked by a "visual symbolic form, for example, a metaphor" (1990, 26). This equating of visual image with metaphor bypasses the issue of juxtaposition of semantic domains. Forms cannot be judged to be metaphorical without the involvement of separate semantic domains; that is, a systematic correspondence between a source domain and a target domain must be clearly established. Brennan notes correctly that the morphemes documented in her data corpus are categorized by similarly motivated forms (e.g., the EMANATE/EMIT morpheme sets).

Brennan makes use of Lakoff and Johnson's experiential theory to define the nature of metaphor: "The essence of metaphor is understanding and experiencing one kind of thing in terms of another" (Lakoff and Johnson 1980, 5, cited in Brennan 1990, 21). She explains that the fully Open (spread) 5 handshape resembles "several long thin things." Thus, "we can see that one set of upright long(-ish), thin(-ish) objects (blades of grass) is represented by another set of upright long(-ish), thin(-ish) objects (fingers)" (1990, 27). This relationship is labeled metaphorical.

However, in the previous example there is no semantic source domain mapping onto a target domain. Clearly, the long, thin fingers *resemble* the blades of grass, suggesting an iconic relationship between the fingers and the blades of grass. No juxtaposition of semantic domains has occurred, which means that the Open 5 handshape is iconic in this instance, rather than metaphorical.

Brennan's Open 5 handshape evoked a symbolic link with the blades of grass. She noted at "a slightly abstract level" that the Open 5 handshape can also be used to symbolize several people

(1990, 27). This Open 5 hand is further extended to represent collections of long thin things that are known in BSL as the "RIVULETS classifier or metaphor" and could be glossed as WATERFALLS, or BLOOD FLOWING. Then at "an even greater degree of abstraction, we can note the abstract notion of 'thought' being expressed in terms of 'lines of thought'" (28).

The BSL sign for "thought" is metaphorical. As in ASL, the sign is articulated near the head, where the thought and cognitive processes are generally associated; the phonological component is the "long, thin, object" handshape. However, it is the relationship between semantic domains that determines metaphoricity with this example, instead of an extended concept of "metaphoricity" (i.e., iconicity) in general.

Brennan recognizes the importance of classifier usage in the productive morphology of BSL, and the way that classifier forms relate to metaphors. She says, "While classifiers need not be metaphorical, in order to carry out their function, in BSL they are for the most part clearly so" (1990, 26). She sees them as "forms which mark out referents as having particular physical or semantic attributes. Because they are primarily associated with physical properties such as shape, size, extent, texture and so on, they can be seen as having most direct application with reference to objects, (including people)" (26). When these morpho-phonemic primes in classifier construction are used to express an abstract concept, they evoke metaphorical referencing. However, Brennan sees this as making use of a "visual metaphor" to express an abstract meaning (1990, 97). This appears to make use of iconic representation rather than metaphorical extension. Thus, a metaphorical expression is correctly documented, but through the use of a broadly based criterion.

Brennan focuses on several prototypical examples of BSL, such as one handshape parameter that expresses what is called the EM-ANATE/EMIT set of morphemes (1990, 96–97). She claims that the opening and closing actions of the hands carry specific types of metaphorical meaning and that this action again demonstrates a visual metaphor. Signs that exploit this underlying visual metaphor include SUN, LIGHT, SEND, TRANSMIT, MAGIC, BOMB, EMIT, SHOUT, and so forth. "Image" is equated with "metaphor" when describing the articulation of these signed words. If a source domain, such as the light paradigm, is used to extend referential mapping to a target domain, such as the abstract notion of magic, then a "visual metaphor" may be correctly assumed. But to label the spreading (iconic) action of the hands as a "basic metaphor" is confusing. Iconic is not necessarily metaphoric.

Brennan suggests it is possible to group individual signs into a set that shares the "same underlying metaphor." She then allows that the "resulting underlying morphemes are productive in that they enter into the word-formation processes of the language" (1990, 124). She notes that the effective communication that is often found among signers of different signed languages may be due to the "shared encoding of visual-spatial relationships and the exploitation of these within metaphor based construction" (1990, 184).

Brennan recognizes the pervasive extent of metaphorical motivation in BSL and the importance of the operation of metaphorical mapping in signed language. "While metaphorically-based morphemes can be used for concrete meanings, metaphors come into their own with respect to the expression of abstract concepts" (1990, 125). If we reexamine her notion of metaphor, especially when it parallels iconicity, we can distinguish explicitly between iconic and metaphoric representations and recognize the important contribution that Brennan has made to the understanding of the metaphorical trope in BSL.

Signed language metaphor has only recently become a focus of linguistic analysis. The iconic shroud that veils metaphorical mapping in signed languages is not easy to remove. When a source domain and a target domain are clearly defined, and the unidirectional mapping is laid out explicitly, the results are clearly metaphorical. We must separate iconicity from metaphor and segregate the important distinctions found in the components of each before we can adequately describe what motivates metaphorical mapping in signed languages. Then the long-standing mystique of metaphor can be revealed, uneclipsed by iconicity.

3

AN ETHNOGRAPHIC
APPROACH TO SIGNED LANGUAGE
DATA COLLECTION

The goal of ethnography is to describe a culture from the native's point of view; the task of ethnographic research is to discover and describe important variables. The initial objective of this study was the elicitation of particular linguistic units, metaphors, rather than a corpus of field notes to be coded ethnographically. However, the ethnographic interview described by Spradley (1979) was the model for the semistructured approach used in this study. Strategies of ethnographic research guided the initial stages of the interviews. Later, an analysis of the collected data revealed patterns that supported the original hypothesis of this study—that American Sign Language (ASL) uses metaphors to talk about language and thought.

The ethnoscientist can begin gathering descriptive information about a topic by asking structured questions to generate "folk terms" for certain domains. This approach may lead to the observation of possible patterns of behavior—in this case, linguistic behavior. The study elicited spontaneous language responses from competent users of ASL, with the idea of exploring the hypothesis that ASL uses metaphorical mapping in language and thought. Informants were asked to respond to proposed metaphors such as THE MIND IS A CONTAINER and THOUGHTS ARE OBJECTS in order to generate and collect a corpus of metaphors in ASL that would lend themselves to linguistic analysis.

To determine the consultants' understanding of metaphorical concepts of communication and thought as used in their own language, a "folk model" was explored. This kind of model involves studying the commonsense understandings shared by everybody in a particular cultural group (D'Andrade 1987, 113). The application of a folk model may reveal a lack of consistency among all the respondents, but the responses obtained are usually based on common experiences of the people who share a language and a culture.

Folk etymologies, a phenomenon discussed in historical linguistics, provide a motivating link for people trying to make sense of the relationship between words and their meanings (Lakoff 1987b). While cautioning that few ordinary persons really know the origin of a word or an expression, Lakoff believes that the folk etymologies that people offer are not just random lists of expressions and associated meanings. They are at least partly inspired by associated conventional images. These images have an important cognitive function: "They make sense of the idioms, and therefore make them easier to understand, learn, remember, and use" (452). There is a psychological validity to the phenomenon of folk etymology; words are easier to learn and remember through its use than through random pairings.

The reliability of folk models and folk etymology can be extended through the use of ethnographic principles. In this study, ethnographic principles guided research inquiry throughout the exploration of metaphorical findings during later in-depth analysis. For example, the folk etymologies from native signers about the phonological verb stem handshape of one of the handle classifiers led to the diachronic examination of the sign GIVE (see chapter 6). This in-depth analysis resulted in the discovery of semantic connections between acts of giving in ASL and in French Sign Language (langue des signes française).

Relying on the intuitive responses of native signers may not be sufficient to ensure accuracy. Native speakers are rarely aware of the principles that structure their language (Lakoff 1987b). It is not a natural language situation to ask informants for grammatical information, and their responses may not always reflect actual language use. As a result, researchers may obtain "an unsystematic perception of usage, colored by social attitudes towards the speech form and even towards the interrogator" (Croft 1990, 26). Linguists wishing to avoid this problem have turned to using textual data in order to provide data that is unfiltered by artificial elicitation situations or by the consultant's self-perceptions.

In the case of ASL, commercial videotaped productions are expensive and time-consuming to preview and transcribe. Videotapes and CD-ROMs have only recently begun to be used to preserve literary excerpts by native signers.[1] However, data from accepted sign language textbooks and commercial videotapes of native signers were used as a resource, supplementing the researcher's own data collection. This adheres closely to Croft's admonition that "no source of data—primary grammars, native informants or actual texts—is perfect; but any and all sources can provide the relevant data when used judiciously" (1990, 26).

Informants and Setting

The majority of consultants for the original study on ASL metaphor were interviewed during the fall of 1990, in Rochester, New York. Four informants were later interviewed in 1991 and 1992, in Albuquerque, New Mexico. All fourteen individuals were either native signers or longtime users (over twenty years) of ASL. They ranged in age from twenty-six to fifty-five years old. All participants signed consent forms and background questionnaires prior to being interviewed and were told that they could stop the interviews at any point. All indicated that they felt most comfortable

---

1. The first widely known filmed passage in sign language was made by the National Association of the Deaf in 1913, when President George Veditz urged "fellow deaf mutes" to "preserve, cherish and defend our lovely sign language" lest it become "taken from" the Deaf community. This film was misplaced in archives until the mid-1970s. Presently, there is only one American Sign Language "epic," videotaped for commercial distribution: "Epic on the Gallaudet Revolution" from *Gilbert Eastman: Live at SMI* (1993), produced by Sign Media, Inc. Ted Supalla, a native ASL signer and a linguist at the University of Rochester, is encouraging archival preservation of historical films and tapes on ASL for linguistic purposes.

using ASL in their daily communications, as opposed to a pidgin mixture of ASL with signed English. All but one of the consultants had graduated from high school. Four held master's degrees, and the rest had either bachelor's degrees or at least one year of experience in college; one holds a doctorate in anthropology.

The consultants had attended high schools across the country: Arizona, California, Indiana, Kansas, Louisiana, Maryland, New Mexico, New York, Oregon, Pennsylvania, and Texas. Five consultants were mainstreamed into the public school systems at one point or another; twelve attended residential schools for the deaf for an average of twelve years each. Two did not attend a residential school at any point in their education; however, both stated that they preferred to use ASL in their daily communication with people.

Six consultants had deaf parents and learned ASL in their home environment. Seven had deaf brothers or sisters, all of whom used ASL to communicate with their siblings. The remaining consultants began learning ASL when entering the residential schools for the deaf by the age of five (except for the two previously mentioned consultants who began learning during their teens).

It was crucial for the consultants in the study to have native or nativelike intuitions about ASL. The use of intuition, a cognitive consideration that advances natural and revealing semantic analysis, helps a speaker to ascertain that "a proposed characterization captures something that he dimly felt but was unable to articulate" (Langacker 1991, 518). Several safeguards were established to ensure that the chosen informants understood and produced the targeted language during the interviews.

Each consultant's language background and general standing in the Deaf community was known by the researcher prior to requesting that the consultants participate in this study. Introductions to consultants in New York were made by a respected intermediary at the chosen site, a culturally accepted hearing professor with deaf parents. Consultants from New Mexico were known and selected by the author. Consultants for subsequent studies that took place in Switzerland, France, and Italy were introduced by established intermediaries from the respective international Deaf communities.

58

Consultants for the original study are respected members of their local communities; several are nationally known in their career areas. Their metalinguistic awareness of ASL appeared to be above average.[2] This opinion is based on the fact that each consultant had participated in various capacities at the postsecondary level of education—through teaching their language and culture, or participating in the training of interpreters who will subsequently use the language in a professional capacity, or through attending and teaching formal seminars and classes conducted in ASL. Due to their general leadership positions, all of the consultants interact with hearing people either through employment, print and broadcast media, or in social situations, and have considerable exposure to English. Therefore, they had acquired a functioning bilingualism through their many contact situations with speakers of English. Until recently the average deaf signer was often unaware that ASL is recognized by linguists to be a natural language. Remarks made throughout the interviews confirmed that each consultant was aware that ASL is considered to be one of the accepted natural languages of the world.

Because what people say and do will vary depending on who is present at the time, it is important to understand one's own impact upon a situation. I have signed for over thirty years, but I am not a native signer of ASL. Therefore, it was appropriate to take into consideration the proficiency of my own signing knowledge since I would interview most of the consultants. I chose to undergo evaluation through the Sign Communication Proficiency Interview (SCPI), an evaluation provided at the National Technical Institute for the Deaf in Rochester, New York. It involves a one-to-one conversation between the interviewer and the candidate, which is videotaped and subsequently rated independently by three SCPI

---

2. One consultant's profile does not fit the characteristics laid out in this paragraph. Metalinguistic understanding of the language, as well as educational background, did not appear to equal that of the average consultant; however, this person's metaphorical and linguistic creativity offered rich data for analysis and was included for that purpose.

raters. The rating in this case was determined to be *superior,* with a functional description of: "Able to use sign vocabulary and grammar with native-like fluency and accuracy for all formal and informal social and work needs. Comprehension, vocabulary, and grammar are excellent."

I have since become an evaluator for the SCPI ratings that take place in New Mexico, as well as for a national evaluating body. Additionally, I am certified as an intermediary interpreter by the national Registry of Interpreters for the Deaf and have been awarded court certification by the New Mexico Administrative Office of the Courts. Therefore, the data collection of interviews can be considered to maintain an accurate reflection of ASL interaction, although it is acknowledged that even greater insights and interaction might have occurred if the interviewer were a native signer also.

The language contact situation between any two signers is complex. Lucas and Valli (1989) have identified almost a dozen language contact possibilities between groups in the American Deaf community. These groups are subdivided according to participant characteristics such as Deaf bilinguals with hearing bilinguals, Deaf ASL monolinguals with hearing bilinguals, Deaf bilinguals with deaf English signers, and so on. They discovered in their research that even native users of ASL choose to communicate with one another in some situations through means "other than ASL" (39). Lucas and Valli discussed a variety of sociolinguistic factors for varying communication patterns. They include a lack of familiarity between participants and a very high level of formality of the situation. In other words, placing two individuals who use ASL as a preferred mode of communication together may not automatically ensure that both participants will use ASL throughout the session.

In this study, each consultant was told prior to the taping of the original interviews that the research session would be conducted in ASL. Manually coded English signing systems are used prevalently in the educational system in the United States, and it was reasonable to predict that elements of these codes would occur during language contact situations. When invented signed representations of English occurred in the interview by the consultant, they were disregarded and were not spiraled back into the conversation by the interviewer. When English structural features that Lucas and Valli call "indigenous, natural signing that occurs as a result of the contact between bilinguals" (1989, 39) occurred, these forms of language usage were accepted as natural interaction to be expected during the session (i.e., partial mouthing of English words, adjective placement that followed English word order on occasions, the literal translation of English idioms or phrases into sign). However, at no point in any of the sessions was spoken English produced.

In addition, at the beginning of most sessions, a "grand tour" question was asked to encourage the consultants to begin thinking metalinguistically about their own language. In ethnographic interviews this type of question allows the consultant to think and elaborate on answers. It can be repeated and rephrased during the interview. In this study, the "grand tour" question was adapted to encourage metalinguistic awareness of the language to be used. Basically, this grand tour question was phrased as follows: In your own opinion, can American Sign Language include components of the English signed systems, or does it strictly distinguish itself from those systems?

In the past, many deaf persons switched to more English-like forms of signed language during formal situations (Fischer 1980). This was due to the traditionally greater acceptance of English and to the rejection of ASL as a natural language. It must be stressed that none of the consultants showed any indication of a denial of the use of ASL. Each proudly used native or near-native ASL fluency while in front of the camera. Videotaped sessions are common experiences in the lives of the individuals chosen as consultants and they appeared comfortable signing before the camera.

Each interview took place in either a quiet, enclosed television studio or a small adapted lecture room at a university. All of the interviews were from thirty to sixty minutes long. During each interview, the only person other than the consultant and the interviewer (researcher or researcher's aide) in the taping room was the camera operator, who was an educator fluent in ASL and who either sat unobtrusively in the background or left during the main portion of the interviews. No interruptions from outsiders took place during the interviews.

Procedures

The consultants were told that the interview would be conducted in ASL and that the topic was the author's research interest—metaphors in ASL. Each person was told that procedural explanations would be provided during the interview itself. The consultants were aware that the interview might run as long as an hour. They were assured that there were no right or wrong answers; the interviewer was simply interested in their opinions and language use. Their responses were allowed to run on for several minutes, until there seemed to be a natural pause and the consultants stopped the response on their own. There was no indication as to whether the interviewer agreed or disagreed with the consultants' contributions. To the contrary, the interviewer encouraged the consultants to feel comfortable with their statements by nodding her head in agreement, smiling as certain points of interest were made, and acknowledging awareness of the subject itself by adding brief comments or questions related to the issue.

The interviewer began the main portion of each interview by briefly defining metaphor. Two main explanations about metaphors were given, one based on the traditional, figurative definition, and the other following the experiential definition of metaphor. Consultants were assured that they did not have to remember, or even comprehend, either of these definitions of metaphors during the interview. This information was presented merely as background.

The consultants were then informed that the interview would focus on the discussion of ASL signs used in two different domains: (1) language and thought and (2) communication and speech (sign) acts. Many of the ASL signs initially presented to the consultants to generate comments were taken from corresponding spoken words discussed and analyzed in Sweetser's (1987b) sources of mental states and speech acts. The words reflected metaphorical mappings in spoken languages derived from general experiential metaphors; for example, see, think, grasp, say. The initial terms generated a revolving, expanding, corpus of data to which the consultants responded. Relevant signs that subsequently occurred in the natural process of the interview were accepted for discussion and focus also. Often, these newly appearing signs were carried over into the following interview for further elaboration by the next consultant.

One of the most frequently asked questions in this study was "Can you sign 'x' (where 'x' equals the targeted gesture) like this?" The initial sign used with each consultant was always a commonly accepted sign, usually from the thought domain such as THINK. Immediately following this question was a demonstration of the targeted sign, produced in isolation, within a phrase, or embedded within a complete sentence. When a consultant acknowledged that the sign used was indeed acceptable in ASL, the sign was frequently articulated in a different location and the same question asked again. The stimulus sign often had only one parameter factor manipulated at a time.[3] During the course of interviews, many signs connected with either thought or communication were generated by the consultants.

Use of this semiethnographically structured approach provided consultants with the opportunity to produce concepts that the researcher had hoped would emerge: metaphorical themes such as **ideas are objects** and **minds are containers**. Without inquiry structure of some kind, it would have been difficult to generate a sufficient corpus of signed concepts needed for the original study.

Consultants often created stories as a means of explaining their reasons for using certain metaphors. Within these narrated explanations, the consultants made use of certain verb forms for depicting that ideas are objects and that these objects can be manipulated. For example, "ideas" accidentally fell from the brain, were found

---

3. ASL signs can be systematically described in terms of formational properties such as handshape, location, movement, and palm orientation (Stokoe, Casterline, and Croneberg 1976; Battison 1978).

clenched within a fist to prevent forgetfulness, or were ejected into space and escaped.

Preliminary analysis of the data began almost concurrently with the first interviews. Numerous references were made to indicate in ASL how ideas travel through the brain and what takes place during the projection of ideas across space to another person's mind. In some cases, the consultants used signs that depicted thoughts as physical objects that were manipulated, thrown, held on to, pooled with other thoughts, and so on.

As the ethnographic interview approach began to generate a promising-looking corpus of ASL signs, other areas for potential analysis began to appear: the phonological form of the generated handshapes, the location and movement patterns and shifts, and the impact of culture upon the comprehension of words used by deaf people. The semantic relationships to the sign parameters (form, location, movements, and palm orientation) began to reveal a need to focus on the reasons behind the variants' metaphorical adaptations and changes—including the systematic use of more standardized, and frozen, signs, and the iconicity revealed within the patterns of use.

The ethnographically structured interviews changed the original inquiry from a search for verification of metaphorical use in ASL to a deeper study of how the form (phonology) of the metaphors motivates the cognitive thinking of the users of ASL. In turn, that study initiated a diachronic investigation that led to a search for grammatical change within signed languages.

Glossing and Depiction of ASL

There is no standardized system for writing ASL that faithfully presents all visual aspects of the essential linguistic components of ASL. Several writing systems have been devised by linguists and others (Newkirk 1987; Stokoe, Casterline, and Croneberg 1976; Sutton 1981), but their systems are not appropriate for this study. Instead, the ASL signs are represented by an English gloss (a rough translation of the ASL term) written in small capital letters. Kegl cautions, however, "It is important to refrain from transferring to a sign the syntactic and semantic characteristics of its English gloss" (1990, 156).

Transcription symbols follow the accepted conventions for detailed diacritics and descriptions found in the field. Transcription formats for metaphors are adapted from the various combinations used by Lakoff and Johnson (1980). English metaphors are indicated through bold lowercase letters, and ASL metaphors are indicated through bold small capital letters.

The ASL model in this book is Keith Cagle, a native signer, the son of Deaf parents. His brother is also a Deaf native signer. He has a master's degree in administration and is working on his doctoral degree in educational linguistics. He reviewed the images of the consultants' data corpus before re-rendering them for the pictures in this book. He is familiar with metaphorical mapping in ASL and has a solid understanding of the topic.

Linguistic Analysis

Linguists seek commonalities from one language to another. By uncovering cross-language patterns we can make sense of our linguistic behaviors. Generative linguistics focuses on "formal grammars," or what Lakoff defined as "systems in which arbitrary symbols are manipulated by rules of a restricted mathematical form without taking into account the interpretation of those symbols" (1990, 43). Cognitive linguistics is concerned with the study of human conceptualization, especially in terms of networks of structures involving categorization. This study has used a cognitive linguistic approach to analysis.

Cognitive linguists share with generative grammarians the concern for systematically describing language structure. Langacker, a leading cognitive linguist, acknowledges that "grammatical patterns and restrictions require explicit characterization" (1991, 534). However, linguistic expressions derive meaning by evoking conceptual content and imposing a particular interpretation of that content. This conceptualization is grounded in bodily experience that is common to all people and that is the basis for interpersonal and intercultural communication. Cognitive linguistic principles are viewed through a unified account both synchronically and diachronically, as compared with a more compartmentalized and mathematically oriented analysis of generative linguistics.[4]

Sweetser looks at the systematicity of semantic changes and claims that there is "coherent, regular structuring within the metaphorical system of interconnections between semantic domains" (1990, 47). To determine this structuring, she works against a backdrop of both synchronic and diachronic structuring of the domains in question. She observes that regularities dealing with the mappings of form to multiple functions cannot be appropriately captured by classical objectivist semantic theory. Instead, regularities are motivated by a cognitively based theory that allows "human perception and understanding of the world to be the basis for the structure of human language" (2).

While working on historical connections between languages, Sweetser noted, "If we are willing to look at such large-scale, systematic historical connections between domains of meaning, it becomes evident that not all of semantic change is as whimsical and perverse as has often been assumed" (1990, 47–48). Sweetser's primary methodology examined meaning changes cross-linguistically and enabled her to observe which senses frequently give rise historically to later senses. She was thereby able to posit close semantic and cognitive links between the senses.

The main hypothesis of this book did not focus on diachronically examined metaphorical mapping of ASL; the data analyzed in chapters 4 and 5 were collected within a time frame of two years. The structured interrelationships between senses or uses of a single word or parameter was examined in all aspects of the studies. Grouping of mappings regularly found by users of ASL was looked at in order to examine motivated accounts of the relationships

---

4. These basic themes fundamental to cognitive linguistics are offered by Diren and Langacker (1990) in their "Call for Contributions" for *Cognitive Linguistics Research in Cognitive Linguistics*.

between senses of a single sign or morpheme. Consultants' accounts of their own earlier use of ASL and perceived historical change of several metaphors is also documented.

Lakoff and Johnson's (1980) theory of experiential metaphorical mapping was the theoretical platform upon which the research for this book was primarily based. Lakoff defined metaphor not as a figure of speech, but as a mode of thought: "a systematic mapping from a source to a target domain" (1990, 50). Lakoff's argument is that human thought processes are largely metaphorical; therefore, studying metaphorical expressions in our everyday language can provide insight into the metaphorical nature of a person's conceptual system.

The relationship between everyday and artistic metaphors reveals complexity and systematicity that is important to both linguists and literary analysts alike: "To the cognitively oriented scholar interested in discovering how poetic metaphor is understood, the conventional foundations and building blocks of creative structures are of essential importance" (Sweetser 1992a, 721). The study of novel metaphors must be based on a sound understanding of the underlying cognitive structural patterns of conventional metaphors.

The everyday language of the communication and thought domains in ASL was subjected to linguistic analysis that follows Lakoff's investigative techniques to determine the expression of metaphorical mapping in ASL. This is in line with Kövecses's proposal for viewing prototypes of cognitive models: one needs to study a large number of conventionalized linguistic expressions that are related to a given concept (1991, 30). The ASL corpus was examined to identify any coherent conceptual structure emerging systematically from the informants' expressions (in language and thought domains) that proved to be metaphorical.

The search for patterns of metaphorical mapping followed an approach referred to as *functionalism*. This particular theory adopts a pragmatic view of language as social interaction and complements the basically ethnographic process used in the collection of the corpus. Croft (1990) says that linguistic structure should be explained primarily in terms of linguistic function. Language structure maximizes functional adaptation within the constraints of the human body and the medium of expression, the case in point being the gestural/visual modality of ASL. Function, especially when communicating meaning in everyday social interaction, is central to this approach.

Throughout the original research interviews, the interviewers asked questions about the function of a word or parameter. For example:

• Why is one sign placed in that particular location?
• Will the meaning change if the sign is moved to a different direction?
• Why was the curvature of the finger made to demonstrate that point?
• How does straightening the bent finger change the meaning of the sign?

These and other similar questions were used to explore the reasoning behind the selection of certain phonological handshapes, specific locations, and path movements that the consultants used when producing their signed responses. Selected expressions and isolated handshape forms that were used metaphorically were identified and categorized.

At the beginning of this chapter it was explained that the initial task of this study was to find and document metaphorical examples in ASL such as THE MIND IS A CONTAINER and THOUGHTS ARE OBJECTS. Cross-linguistic comparison of metaphorical concepts has shown that spoken languages commonly express this fundamental cognitive phenomenon (metaphorical mapping). Identification of the cognitive conceptualization in ASL indicates the irrelevancy of modality where the existence of metaphorical mapping is concerned.

Another research question emerged as the interviews progressed. This had to do with one of the handshape variants of the ASL sign TO-GIVE. The sign arose in the discussions dealing with thought and language; its predicate verb stem handle was used to manipulate and move ideas. As mentioned previously, a folk theory about the etymology of one of the GIVE variants made by many of the consultants initiated a research tangent that resulted in the investigation of grammatical connections between ASL and French Sign Language.

Ultimately, the analysis broadened into a study of cross-linguistic cultural impacts that metonymy and metaphor have on various groups of signed language users. Showing visual instantiations of selected metaphors and metonyms to native and nativelike users of ASL, Swiss German Sign Language, and Italian Sign Language resulted in distinct cultural interpretations of the tropes. The cross-linguistic and cross-cultural commonalities and differences found in the intertropic contiguity of a poem are analyzed in chapter 7.

In summary, the theoretical frameworks of experiential cognitive researchers documented in chapter 1, along with a complementary functional approach to the analysis of the data, provides a foundation for the hypothesis that ASL uses metaphors to talk about language and thought. Subsequent discovery of metaphors in ASL enabled the author to push the study further. By making use of the folk theories generated about the history of certain handshapes, the study led to the identity of a diachronic line of lexicalization that takes place in the sign GIVE. Cross-linguistic language patterns and cultural distinctions emerged following the discussions of a signed poem with intertropic instantiations.

The semiethnographic analysis used to generate ASL data has resulted in a methodology that can be used by other ASL researchers to study the intertropic relationship of simile, metonymy, metaphor, and the cross-linguistic and cross-cultural use of these tropes.

4

REVIEWING THE TROPES IN
AMERICAN SIGN LANGUAGE

Metaphors and related tropes interact with, are embedded within, and heavily motivate and influence, each other. While each trope involves psychologically distinct cognitive processes, their interaction is intertwined in deep and subtle ways. The analysis of ASL metaphors helps to delineate these relationships.

To understand what something is, it helps to determine what it is not. In this chapter an ASL metaphor is distinguished from two other major tropes in ASL, simile and metonymy. The analysis of ASL metaphors is basically two-pronged: (1) identifying expressions of metaphorical themes related to language and thought domains and (2) analyzing handshapes that lend themselves to metaphorical construes via their phonological forms and productive morphemes within the signs.

Metaphorical Mapping

Lakoff and colleagues' cognitive framework of metaphorical mapping in spoken languages shows that the conceptual system is grounded in experience. In ASL there is additional complexity in how metaphors are mapped. The mapping found in ASL reveals not only the iconicity prevalent in spoken languages (Armstrong 1983; Bybee 1985; Fauconnier 1985; Fleischman 1989; Givón 1991; Haiman 1985; Langacker 1991; Talmy 1983), but also the use of handshape icons (and their corresponding movements and locations) that add their own visual images to the linguistic spectrum.[1]

ASL phonemes and morphemes can be isomorphic, with their corresponding handshapes having the same appearance of form. As Gee and Kegl state, "The isomorphism between ASL's formational (phonetic) component, its morphology and its semantics gives us a window onto the semantics of natural language and meaning previously limited to the realm of speculation" (1982, 199).[2] Although the phonological and the morphological properties of ASL may, at times, be one and the same, it is important to recognize the difference between iconic and metaphorical conceptual relationships. The examples given in figures 4, 5, and 6 highlight this difference.

Figure 4 depicts an iconic representation of a container (as opposed to a metaphorical concept) in ASL. The ASL model demonstrates an isomorphic use of a cupped hand to show, through mimetic behavior, the brain of an individual who was fatally damaged in a car accident.[3] The cupped hand indicates the approximate size of the brain and skull that was being described. The source of the imitation was a brain seen by a consultant earlier in a videotaped movie. This imitation of a person's skull and brain matter is purely isomorphic—the cupped hand represents a visual approximation of the skull that was flapped up and off of the victim's brain. There is a direct visual similarity between the size and shape of the hands and the skull being discussed. The source of the imagery is the skull seen on the videotape; the cupped handshape is

---

1. Icons such as handshapes are semantically influenced by accompanying variations of movement and locations. Nonmanual grammatical markings are also frequently essential to the semantic polysemy of many signs; however, they are not the direct focus of this analysis. It should be recognized, nevertheless, that future work on metaphors will most certainly uncover facial grammatical markings that motivate metaphoricity.

2. In the same work, Gee and Kegl (1982, 209) also state, "The morphological representations given for ASL can be considered morphophonemic representations as well because each phoneme is also a morpheme. In fact, it is this property that in part allows the morphological structure of ASL to mediate a virtual isomorphism between its phonetics and its semantics."

3. I am indebted to Keith Cagle for serving as the ASL model in this book.

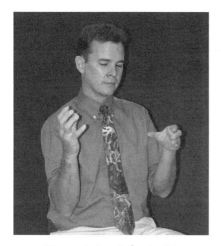

Figure 4. Iconic brain #1

Figure 5. Iconic brain #2

Figure 6. Metaphorical brain

simply a signed representation for the damaged skull being discussed. There is no crossing of conceptual domains in producing this iconically represented concept.

A second source of isomorphic iconicity occurred in the data when a consultant was describing the work of a mortician's aide. Parts of the skull, including the smooth sheen of the dura, were being described. Once again, a container handshape was produced.

In figure 5, note a simple iconic representation of a portion of a skull being held after the brain had been dissected. The consultant showed the top of the skull as it was about to be placed back onto the top of the brain following the autopsy. The source of the imagery is a brain; the signed representation is once again the brain. The consultant produced a simple isomorphic depiction of the shape of the container (skull) that he was describing.

These two examples above describe similar size and shape specifiers that represent iconic images of brains or skulls. In figure 6, another classifier handshape is pictured. The phonological components look identical, with one hand depicting the shape of a container and the other hand forming the similar lid handshape found in the previous examples. However, this representation is metaphorical. A consultant explained that some people enjoy teasing others. For example, if a friend has been thinking dirty or lascivious thoughts, it might be wise to remove the person's skull lid and give the entire inside of the brain a thorough deep-cleaning. Then, after the cleansing, the person can revert back to a more virtuous state of pious thinking.

Because the classifier handshape used for this metaphorical skull is similar to the shape specifier used in the previous two examples, there is, of course, iconic depiction involved. Once again, the source in this example is an actual brain. However, the target is a container conceptualized by the consultant to hold immaterial substance—lewd thoughts. No one can physically pick up ideas or wash them away. They are abstract, without a physical structure of their own. This places the target in a separate domain—a domain of abstraction that is different from the source domain of physical substance. The cupped hands become an abstract container for thoughts and ideas, not the depiction of a physical brain (or skull) being manipulated. Thus, figure 6 is metaphorical, as well as iconic.

The spatial structure seen in this container schema substantiates Lakoff's Spatialization of Form hypothesis—"image schemas (which structure space) are mapped into the corresponding abstract configurations (which structure concepts)" (1987a, 283). There is a metaphorical mapping of the image schema of a physical container onto a conceptual structure filled with abstract thoughts and ideas; a concrete domain is metaphorically projected onto an abstract domain.

Thus, the conventional metaphor found in English, **the mind is a container,** is substantiated in ASL also. The mind can be conceived of as a dynamic container filled with intellectual activities and locative relationships, regardless of the linguistic modality being utilized. The illustration of the container schema and its related THE MIND IS A CONTAINER metaphor described above helps to distinguish between iconic and metaphorical sign usage. In the discussion of the following metaphorical concepts, iconic representation is still quite noticeable but is often used as a vehicle for metaphoricity— the crossing of distinct domains.

The matrix in table 2 helps to describe and distinguish concepts of iconicity and metaphoricity found in ASL. The four quadrants show the interdependency of icons and metaphors. Examining the C classifiers (classifiers made with a C handshape) in figures 4 and 5, we see that the first two examples for BRAIN fall into Quadrant #2 because the shapes in the source domains (damaged brain image seen on videotape / dissected brain) are iconic, and the target domains (brain being signed and discussed / brain being signed and discussed) are also simply iconic representations of physical objects. There is no crossing of conceptual domains here. Therefore, the status of the components are iconic rather than metaphorical.

The brain image in figure 6, however, falls within Quadrant #1, since the iconic cupped hands in the source domain (the image of skull) and the target domain (the conceptual container filled with abstract thoughts) are two separate domains—one concrete, the other abstract. The brain represents the mind, which is the locus of

Table 2. Relationship between Iconicity and Metaphoricity

	Metaphoric	
	+	−
Iconic +	1	2
Iconic −	3	4

thoughts. Quadrant #1 encompasses both iconicity and metaphoricity.[4]

In the following sections, iconicity is often explicitly evoked due to the isomorphic handshapes that are necessary to produce the signed words. ASL is not unique in its iconic cognitive framework; it is also prevalent in spoken languages. Prior research on metaphor in ASL has been systematically confounded by the issue of iconicity, so it is important to identify and to distinguish iconicity from metaphoricity when analyzing the ASL metaphors (see chapter 5 for further discussion of signs within the quadrants).

Related Tropes in ASL

Simile

The *New Collins Concise Dictionary of the English Language* offers a simple definition for this trope: "A simile is an expression which describes one person or thing as being similar to another." *Webster's Ninth New Collegiate Dictionary* states that simile is distinguished from metaphor "in that the comparison is made explicit." Lexical terms such as *like* or *as* introduce similes. Examples of English similes are **She runs like a deer** and **He's as white as a sheet.** In ASL, when two unlike things are compared in order to point out the similarity between them, the signer uses a sign that can be glossed into English as LIKE or SAME AS (see fig. 7). This sign is used explicitly for the purpose of expressing similitude.

The same issues that clouded the distinction between metaphor and iconicity seem to affect the distinction between metaphor and simile. What was originally conceived as a simple categorizational effort in order to show the contrast between metaphor and simile became a more complicated analytical task. Some examples from the data that appear to be similes are discussed below. It should be stressed that the analysis of simile in

---

4. Readers may want to review O'Brien's (1999) work on separating iconicity from metaphoricity. In that psycholinguistic experience, DOLL would be included in Quadrant #4 due to its metaphoric and iconic arbitrariness.

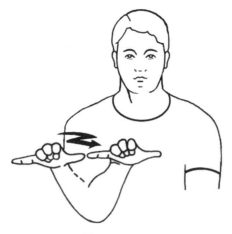

Figure 7. LIKE

ASL is at an initial stage. Others who wish to examine this complex trope in ASL will want to expand upon the discussion offered in this section.

The search for a simile in ASL was based upon three criteria:

1. the definition of an expression that described someone or something as being similar to someone or something else;
2. Halliday's stipulation that the resemblance be explicitly signaled by a tag sign such as LIKE or AS (1985, 319–20); and
3. the requirement that the comparison be explicit rather than implicit.

In the data, an ASL simile of the following linguistic structure was identified:

Simile: [concept————-*LIKE*————-concept]

An ASL simile makes use of what is also the typical English simile structure exemplified in a sentence such as ***The child is like a rambunctious puppy dog.*** This type of sentence stresses how the child is playing, through the use of the phrase introduced by what is also recognized as a simile indicator, the word *like*. An example of an ASL simile [concept————-*LIKE*————-concept] is discussed below. Several relevant tropic concepts discovered within the simile are shown in figure 8.

The consultant noted that interpreters seem to be quite interested in discussing the mental process of interpretation. He elaborated by saying that his interpreter friends had confided that the thought process required while voice interpreting could be com-

OPEN-DRAWER   RIFLE-THROUGH

PULL-OUT

Figure 8. FILE CABINET simile

pared to rifling through a file cabinet. The segment is glossed as: *MENTAL PROCESS, WHILE INTERPRETING, TALK, LIKE, OPEN-FILE-CABINET-DRAWER, RIFLE-THROUGH, PULL-OUT, EXPRESS.*[5] Broadly translated into English: "When an interpreter is performing sign-to-voice interpretation, the mental process involved is *like* rifling through the various folders in a file cabinet before determining which one will be taken out and used."

Although more complex than the simple English example (*the child is like a puppy dog*), the ASL simile structure follows the same syntactic order: an initial concept is joined by the simile indicator LIKE and is followed by the concept being compared. However, this example also vividly demonstrates how intertwined simile, metonymy, and metaphorical concepts can be.

The featured tropic component (OPEN-FILE-CABINET-DRAWER, RIFLE-THROUGH, PULL-OUT) is a complex example of the use of an ontological metaphor at the basic level, **the mind is an entity**. Specifically, metaphor at the subordinate level deals with memory as a storehouse of object-ideas. Grasping the handle of the file cabinet drawer represents the use of a metonymic (synecdoche) component. There is also a basic-level metaphor from the category **ideas are objects subjected to physical force**. (These metaphors are expanded further in the following chapter.)

Thus, in this attempt to identify a simple simile, complex clusters of metaphors and metonyms are found to be linked by the tag sign LIKE. It requires analysis of several different tropes in order to analyze this one simile. It also raises questions: Does simile encompass both metaphor and metonymy; or is simile merely a linking of metaphorical and metonymic clusters?

---

5. Glossed translations are of the manual signs only. Nonmanual facial expressions, which are complex and, admittedly, add essential grammatical information, will not be glossed unless specifically indicated. Glossing grammatical facial markings is beyond the scope of this book. However, the subsequent "broad" translations will attempt to include interpretation of facial grammar and other relevant nonmanual information, as well as the manual content.

A second example of an ASL simile is shown in figure 9. This sentence is glossed as *INDEX LIKE TRAIN*. The broad translation is: "The mental process of interpreting is just like a train."

The consultant first indexes to the center, thereby mentally establishing a referent in the signing space. In this case, the indexed reference was the topic that immediately preceded the glossed seg-

INDEX   *LIKE*

TRAIN

Figure 9. TRAIN simile

ment—the mental process of interpretation. Indexing is considered by Langacker (1991) to be *iconicity of instantiation*. An instance is thought of as having a particular location in the domain of instantiation. This particular domain is one in which an entity is thought of as residing or having its primary manifestation. Langacker sees *time* as the domain of instantiation for events, and *space* for material substances. Thus, the simile in figure 9 indicates that the mental process of interpretation is (metaphorically) considered to be an abstract entity that can be indicated by indexing toward its domain of instantiation. While indexing, the consultant was also supporting Liddell's spatial image referencing, as described in chapter 2 (1990).

After INDEX, the simile indicator LIKE is articulated, followed by the citation sign for TRAIN.[6] Once again, the initial concept precedes the LIKE tag and is immediately followed by the concept being compared. This ASL simile also follows the same word order found in conventional English similes.

One consultant, while discussing simile structure in ASL, stressed that the tag LIKE cannot be articulated before the second concept is produced, since there is nothing in place to refer to yet. While this is a valid and sensible observation, ASL simile is nevertheless noted in the data and represents a common syntactic structure found in ASL discourse[7] (see figs. 8 and 9). However, acting on this informant's observation and concern, further analysis revealed a "simile-like" phenomenon that actually described identity.

Identity: [concept———concept———*LIKEx*]

This grammatical structure meets two of the designated criteria for determining simile: resemblance is explicitly signed by a tag sign

---

6. Immediately following this simile structure, the informant signed two vehicle classifiers (CL:3), placing them one after another directly over his head. This suggested an interpretation that the sign TRAIN represented abstract thoughts linked up together, following one after another in conceptual sequence during thought processing.

7. Another example of the LIKE appearing before the simile's second concept is produced occurs when using the common "YOU KNOW, LIKE . . ." in a topic/comment sentence structure. See Janzen's (1998) dissertation on this subject for more analysis.

such as LIKE or SAME AS, and the comparison is explicit rather than implicit. However, the description of the characteristics involved seems to be one of *identity* rather than *similarity*. Also, the LIKEx tag used when identifying *exactness* as opposed to *similarity* undergoes an inflectional change. For example, the first concept is set up in a designated site somewhere in the signer's space. The second concept, which makes reference to an identical object or abstraction (map, car, idea, or so forth) is signed at a different location. The informant then places the LIKEx tag (the Y handshape without the side-to-side movement of the LIKE tag) at the first concept site, then lifts it and moves it precisely on top of the location of the second concept—indicating an exact identity between the two concepts. A different sentence structure is produced by varying the spatial aspect. Thus, when identical (as opposed to similar) concepts are being compared, it is not possible—as the consultant astutely noticed—to use the simile syntactic structure.

Just as the English language conveys similarity in many different ways, including the use of metaphor (e.g., "He's a dog"; "He looks like a dog"; "He's like a dog"; "He is your puppy dog"), several degrees of similarity can be conveyed in ASL. Disregarding the identity structure described above, the data reveal that ASL simile uses at least two additional LIKE tag variants:

variant A   [concept——*LOOKS-LIKE*——concept]
variant B   [concept——*MORE-LIKE*——concept]

LOOKS-LIKE is a compound of FACE and SAME; MORE-LIKE depicts comparable similarity. Both function within the described ASL simile structure [concept——*LIKE*——concept]. There may be other LIKE tag markers that reveal additional degrees of similitude, as well as other simile sentence structures. It may be possible that specific signs found in the lexicon of ASL, such as PARALLEL or PROPORTIONAL, also convey similitude.

The ASL simile segment shown in figure 10 demonstrates the linguistic complexity found in ASL discourse.[8] While the example is complicated due to turn-taking that occurred between the consultant and the interviewer, other similar simile segments have been

| PICTURE | LIKE | SPARKLE |

| STARS | SMOKE | TOUCH-UP |

Figure 10. ASL "cartoon" simile segment

found that also raise the question of further complexity of this trope. The topic being discussed in figure 10 is whether ideas can be metaphorically manipulated. The consultant explains that ideas can be rejected and discarded. The interviewer interrupts by asking whether ideas can be moved. The consultant stresses that they can be, then pauses, looks to the left, and signs PICTURE, C-A-R-T-O-O-N,

---

8. Still frames from the videotaped discourse cannot capture the virtuosic signing that is simplistically glossed as SPARKLE, STARS, SMOKE in figure 10. The photographs represent a primitive attempt to convey complex handshapes, paths, and movements found within the lexical envelope of the three signs.

LIKE, SPARKLE, STARS, SMOKE, TOUCH-UP, MOVE₁, MOVE₂, NICE, PERFECT. The
following broad translation picks up the previous topic of discussion—that ideas can be moved—and incorporates it into the holistic
simile *"We see the same thing in a cartoon that has images of ideas
inside the bubble—flashing about like glistening lights and popping
sparklers—until the thoughts are placed exactly the way the mind
wishes them to be, arranged just so, with all thoughts coherent and
whole."*

In this complex simile, a general concept is first indicated (PIC-
TURE), then a specific concept (C-A-R-T-O-O-N) is specified through
the use of fingerspelling.[9] The simile indicator LIKE connects several
specific visual images (SPARKLE, STARS, SMOKE) of the dynamic
thoughts found in a cartoon bubble in order to refer back to the
prior question from the interviewer, "Can ideas be moved?" It is
a complex simile that involves not only [concept——LIKE——
concept], but also the topic discussed prior to the point of interrup-
tion by the interviewer. The eye shifts, pauses, and facial markings
found within figure 10 are additional grammatical markings that
may also motivate simile in ASL.

Another example of what may be a complex form of simile (or
even a type of metaphor since there is no accompanying LIKE tag) is
found in Clayton Valli's poem "Lone Sturdy Tree."[10] The poem depicts how the poet, at an earlier age, related his relentless struggle
with teaching in the hearing world to the survival of a rugged,
crusty pine that he spied at the top of a rolling mountainside on the
side of the highway. The lone pine had no shelter or protection
from the natural elements and, though bent and beaten by the
storms and wind, had nevertheless managed to persevere and to
survive. Valli shows through the use of eye gaze, pause, and head

9. For more information on fingerspelling, see Groode (1992), Patrie (1997),
and Wilcox (1992).

10. This poem is part of a video series of American Sign Language poetry
produced by Sign Media, Inc., called *Poetry in Motion*. The author signs the original poem, then discusses why it was created, its form and structure, and its hid-
den meanings and messages.

turn, a possible simile that is void of the signed simile indicator LIKE. The question to be determined is whether this excerpt is a simile or, because it lacks a LIKE tag, a metaphor. There is also indication, due to the contiguity involved, of the intertwining of metonymic concepts (see next section).

The same identity issue arises in English, with the assertion that A = B is a metaphor, yet, A = *like* B is a simile. Examine the sentence **John is a rock.** This is accepted as a classic metaphorical statement. However, the sentence *John is like a rock* is commonly labeled a simile, due to the simple insertion of the indicator *like.* It may be that a greater differentiation can be made between the two tropes. When Valli describes the similarity between the tree and his younger self, he specifies certain referents that are then cognitively set in the mind of the viewer. Although there is no actual manual production of the sign LIKE, any interpretation of the poem must take into consideration the point that Valli is discussing the similarities between certain characteristics of his spirit and the physical condition and longevity of the tree. One reading could be the underlying meaning of the whole poem: "I am *like* that tree in certain specified ways."

On the other hand, the poet may be offering, "I am that tree" or "That tree is me." Are these metaphorical readings different from the so-called simile reading in the above paragraph? The lack of a traditional simile indicator in this ASL poem indicates the need for further exploration of simile production in ASL. Instead of only a simple distinction between the two tropes—the insertion of LIKE— it is possible that simile structures may also be motivated by limited and specified references (eye gaze, pauses, nonmanual markings, etc.), whereas metaphorical references are less clearly specified.

Kittay states, "Simile accomplishes some of the same cognitive ends [as metaphor], but uses different linguistic resources" (1987, 143). Typically, it is thought that the "different linguistic resources" in English refer to indicators such as the words *like* or *such as.* It can been seen from figure 10 and Valli's ASL example above, however, that eye gazes or spatial body stances may also communicate similitude and are examples of different linguistic resources in ASL worthy of further investigation.

Although Davidson admits that "a simile wears a declaration of similitude on its sleeve," he sees further distinction between metaphor and simile: "We might then say the author of simile intended us—that is, meant us—to notice that similarity. But having appreciated the difference between what the words meant and what the author accomplished by using those words, we should feel little temptation to explain what has happened by endowing the words themselves with a second, or figurative meaning" (Davidson 1981, 210). In other words, the simile creator wishes the receiver to limit understanding of content to the references explicitly indicated through the simile structure. The creator of a metaphor, on the other hand, allows the receiver freer cognitive reign over the referents available for comprehension.

Although it can be argued that Valli's poem is full of metaphorical expressions, it is nevertheless obvious that the references toward self and tree were clearly indicated (even without the LIKE sign) and further references generating *differences* are not explicitly offered. Metaphors are mapped according to culturally understood experiential mappings that abound in Valli's poem (e.g., working and living in a hearing-dominated culture). The limiting scope of references between Valli and the tree demands that simile be considered, however. Mac Cormac says that while a consideration of differences is not prohibited, there is less inclination to search into cognitive possibilities when a simile indicator encourages the spotlighting of similarities only (1985, 35).

In ASL, a simile indicator of whatever nature—eye gaze, pause, spatial organization and phrase order, and discourse content—should be investigated in order to distinguish between simile and metaphor. Psycholinguistic experiments in which carefully examined cases with almost identical texts (one with and one without possible simile indicators) need to be examined for different possible interpretations.

Searle recognizes the complexity of similitude: "The problem of metaphor is either very difficult or very easy. If the simile theory were true, it would be very easy, because there would be no separate semantic category of metaphor—only a category of *elliptical utterances* where 'like' or 'as' had been deleted from the uttered sentence. But alas, the simile theory is not right, and the problem of metaphor remains very difficult" (1986, 103). Taking a broader viewpoint regarding simile and metaphor, Lakoff and Turner say, "Statements of both forms can employ conceptual metaphor. The kind called a simile simply makes a weaker claim. . . . On the whole, the syntactic form of an utterance has little, if anything, to do with whether metaphor is involved in comprehending it" (1989, 132).

The literature on simile in spoken languages shows many conflicting theories (Basso 1976; Chiappe 1998; Davidson 1981; Goossens 1990; Kittay 1987; Lakoff and Turner 1989; Mac Cormac 1985; Searle 1986; Pesmen 1991) with no real consensus as to what constitutes this tropic behavior. Indeed, Chiappe refers to similarity as a "highly unstable relation" (1998, 17), thereby making it difficult to use as a basis for examining metaphor and other tropic processes. Whether similes in ASL stand on specific grammatical structure and metaphors do not still needs to be studied. A cognitive function so similar to metaphor cannot be disregarded. When initiating this look at simile, it was my intention to cursorily point out the difference (if any) from metaphor. Instead, it was discovered that simile in ASL deserves more extensive examination than this chapter can provide. Yet the few examples illustrated in this section indicate that discoveries in ASL may lead to further information on the pervasive and subtle similarities—or differences—between these two tropes.

Metonymy in ASL

Whereas a metaphor is a way of achieving understanding principally through conceiving of one thing in terms of another, metonymy has a referential function and allows us to use one entity to stand for another (Lakoff and Johnson 1980, 36). Not only is a part selected to stand for the whole, but a particular characteristic of the whole is selected that will function to highlight further understanding. This continuity allows cognitive movement from a concrete entity to an abstract one, or from an abstract process to a concrete object.

Lakoff and Johnson provide an example of metonymy in spoken English: *"The Times* has not yet arrived for the press conference" (1980, 36–37). This allows conceptualization of one thing by means of its relation to another. *"The Times"* not only refers to some reporter who had not arrived, but further suggests the importance of the institution that the reporter represents. In other words, *"The Times* has not yet arrived" means something different from "Steve Roberts has not yet arrived," even though Steve Roberts may be the *Times* reporter in question.

Metonymic representation is one way in which signs can be nonarbitrary in structure. "Many constructions in ASL may be viewed as a mapping of continuous code elements onto continuous real-world phenomena" (DeMatteo 1977, 6). Friedman points out that "no accurate description of ASL phonological structure can fail to take into account the pervasive use of nondiscrete and iconic (nonarbitrary) elements" (1977, 7).

In ASL, Mandel (1977) distinguished between direct iconic representation (e.g., the drawing of an outline of a common object; pointing to the nose for the sign NOSE) and nondirect representation by classic part-to-whole metonymy. Metonymic concepts are grounded in our experience and structure our language and thoughts, just as metaphors do. However, Lakoff and Johnson stress that a metonymic concept is generally more obvious "since it usually involves direct physical or causal associations" (1980, 40).

There are many metonymical signs in ASL in which a part represents the whole through nondirect representation. HORSE, BUNNY, and COW are examples of words in which body parts (ears or horns) that resemble the physical attributes being graphically articulated are used to specify the entire animal. The ear of a bunny metonymically represents the whole rabbit through synecdoche, or a part-to-whole relationship. The icon of a hand representing what looks like a rabbit's ear is an instantiation of iconicity.

THREE-O'CLOCK, one of a set of number-incorporated time signs, originates at the top of the wrist, the typical location for a wristwatch (see fig. 11). Although it is difficult to know the origin of this

Figure 11. THREE-O'CLOCK

particular set of time indicators, it is probably safe to assume that their emergence in ASL coincided with the emerging use of wristwatches in the early 1900s.[11] This would indicate that wristwatch number incorporated time signs (WNITS) represent a relatively new categorization of time signs. The fact that the top of the wrist is lightly touched before indicating the hour is not arbitrary. In ASL, WNITS are conceived of in terms of the location of a wristwatch. When articulating a WNITS, the particular spot is touched whether a wristwatch is worn or not. A coherent set of time signs are characterized by the site of an initial contact point. Touching the designated spot also serves to focus on the metonymic aspect of the sign. A further metonymic extension allows the mechanism within the watch to stand for the concept of time itself.

The fact that a signer points to the spot on the wrist to indicate time has to do with the cultural use of wristwatches in our society. The prevalence of people who use wristwatches probably indicates

---

11. Handbooks, or "dictionaries," of signed languages compiled by Long (1918), Higgins (1923), and Michaels (1923) do not show examples of this time set. All three picture or describe a more generic time-sign for "period" or "era." Long describes, and Higgins illustrates, a TIME sign in which the dominant index finger taps the top of the nondominant wrist. There are no numerical values incorporated into the production of any of these early ASL signs.

the importance of time in our society. Hands are also highly visible and usually uncovered. Therefore, it is logical for a time indicator to be found on that particular location on our bodies, as opposed to some other arbitrary spot on the body. Cultural experiences having to do with the location of a wristwatch created a conceptual category that motivated a whole new set of time signs.

Wilbur uses the sign for COFFEE (see fig. 12) in referring to the use of part of an object or action as a reference for the whole, even if the coffee being discussed is instant or drip (1987, 165). In this sign, the two hands interact, with the dominant hand shaped like a fist making a circular motion, vividly representing the turning of the handle of an old-fashioned coffee grinder. The nondominant hand, also in the shape of a fist, is a stationary icon for the bottom part that metonymically represents the coffee mill container.

The A_s classifiers (fist handshapes) are part of the predicate classifier subsystem in ASL. Grasping the "handle" creates a part-to-whole synecdoche in which the handle stands for the entire coffee grinder. The grip on the handle can expand to act as a metonym for separate part-to-whole extensions: the nominal coffee grinder handle, the beverage, the substance being ground, and the grinding activity. The iconic circular movement of the handle assumes linguistic aspects, depending on the discourse and the inflection of the movement. The slower, larger movements represent verbal activity;

Figure 12. COFFEE

the rapid, smaller circling motions are the structural expression of the nominalized form.

The encyclopedic model of metonymy is exemplified by the elaboration of various representations across conceptual domains (Croft 1991). COFFEE can be elaborated to mean the beans; a certain kind of ice cream or candy; a dark, rich coloring, a particular type of break at a work station; or the plant itself. The grinding motion highlights a process for the substance (beans) worked upon, rather than alternative possibilities: growing, roasting, or drinking the coffee. Thus, the handle grip is a complex metonymical extension for the noun coffee and its many extensions, as well as the verb activity created by the movement of the handshape icons.

Another example of metonymy also includes metaphor in its analysis. The ASL sign PRESIDENT is commonly recounted as having originated from the two-handed signs representing "the horns of authority" and "the horns of a bull."[12] There is no way to evaluate the accuracy of this folk model, since ASL is not a written language; as a result, tracing the early etymology of ASL words is difficult. However, if we follow the folk etymology commonly cited, two cognitive rationales present themselves. In the first, the horns

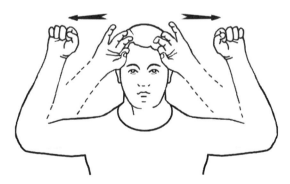

Figure 13. PRESIDENT

---

12. Folk etymology also reveals another possibility for the origin of this sign: George Washington's tricornered hat. However, Long's description of grasping "imaginary horns" (1918, 104) led the analysis to focus on the horn example.

metonymically (part-for-whole) represent the head of the animal, which further extends to represent the entire animal (bull). In the second, specified referents that make up the concept for "bull" are then metaphorically extended to represent PRESIDENT. Thus, we see that the sign is an icon for HORNS; HORNS is a metonym for "bull"; "bull" is a metaphor for PRESIDENT. The subjectification principle described by Langacker (1990, 1991) is exemplified by this cognitive shift from the physical to the abstract.

Although both lexical items represent animate objects, the source domain, horns of a bull, offers several referents accepted by the target domain, PRESIDENT. An icon for the concrete physical horns of the animal metaphorically comes to represent the authoritarian figure that a president represents through the following referents: (1) the leadership image of the bull with his herd in the meadow; (2) the strength and size of the bull represents the power and status of the president; (3) the notion that a bull is not something that can be ignored. The bull is respected, whether for its strength, its established position as a leader, or its sheer size. These folk notions of the concept of a bull are typically mapped onto someone who assumes the presidential role of a body of people. Some conflicting and contradicting ideas, of course, temper the weight of the metaphor. We know that a president is elected; therefore, the presidential power comes not from brute force, but from the collective power of the body politic. This, as well as the fact that a president can be small in physical stature—and need not even be male—limits our mapping of the concept of a bull onto that of PRESIDENT. However, even with this fairly simple metonymic (and metaphoric) concept, we see the highlighting and hiding of referents according to environmental and cultural influences.

Lakoff and Johnson (1980) claim that metonymic concepts, like metaphorical concepts, are grounded in our experience. The part-for-whole metonymy emerges from our experiences the way parts in general are related to wholes. A steering wheel is experientially grounded as a device for causing movement through control. Grabbing on to the steering wheel of a moving car can cause the vehicle to be spun around, driven safely for hundreds of miles, and so on.

The variety of movement that the steering wheel of a car affords is illustrated in a grammatically productive way. Basso states that the use of metaphor exhibits "that kind of creativity which consists of the discovery of possibilities implicit in a [linguistic] system, but not yet discovered, not yet known" (1976, 116). Johnson claims that our understanding of a situation involves "bodily orientations, perceptions, and actions that have *linguistic* [italics added] and cultural dimensions" (1987, 103).

This linguistic motivation is seen in the analysis of DRIVE (see fig. 14). In ASL, the sign is produced by the two hands first grasping an imaginary steering-wheel of a car. This verb DRIVE can be nominalized into the ASL sign CAR by a process involving movement change.[13] Both words become metonymic concepts, in which the part stands for the whole.

Two hands grasped in the signing space do not represent the steering wheel alone. The holding and steering motions metonymically stand for the entire car, which is being driven, turned, or stopped. The part of the car selected for this metonymic function—the steering wheel—provides a referential function common in all

Figure 14. DRIVE

---

13. Supalla and Newport (1978) discuss noun/verb pair distinction. Nominals are distinguished by constrained movements of the hands.

metonymic concepts: it becomes a device that allows conceptualization of one thing by means of its relation to something else. In other words, there could have been other functions or characteristics of a car—the adjustment of the rearview mirror, the spinning wheels, the entering of the vehicle—that served as an identifying reference.

The steering wheel is not a simple metonym, nor is it merely a pantomimic gesture. Due to the richness of the chosen metonymic referent (the steering wheel), ASL users have been able to map rich linguistically productive properties of temporal aspect, manner, and agent behavior onto this metonymic sign. Using highly specified path movements (Klima and Bellugi 1979) that operate in specific predictable ways—circular reduplicated, elliptical reduplicated, single quick thrustlike, single accelerating movement, for example—a signer can indicate a great deal of information such as how long, how fast, or how carefully the vehicle is being driven. Other grammatical information such as the direction and the agent can also be incorporated into the sign through specific path or deictic movements.

The productive richness of this metonymic reference can be explained in terms of Lakoff and colleagues' experiential metaphorical basis for cognitive thinking: we make use of the patterns from our daily physical activities to organize more abstract reasoning. Holding on to the steering wheel probably represents the most physical relationship that we typically have with a vehicle, since sitting is not very experiential. The interaction is personal, manipulative, and ultimately, linguistically complex. The complexity is due to the highly experiential connection that we have with our automobiles. This metonymic synecdoche correlates our abstract cognitive reasoning with the physical grounding of a common experience. It serves to focus specifically on certain referenced aspects of our conceptual information regarding the whole.

Cumulative Metaphtonymy

The Deaf community has been described as a group of people with a cultural base, with many values and mores different from those of the hearing society (Lane 1984; Lane et al. 1996; Lucas 1989; Mow 1989; Padden 1980; Padden and Humphries 1988; Rutherford 1988, 1989; Wilcox 1989; Wilcox and Wilcox 1997). There is a sign in ASL that is simultaneously metaphorical and metonymic. It illustrates the powerful conflicting cultural influences experienced by Deaf persons through their interactions with non-Deaf persons: THINK-HEARING (see fig. 15).

THINK-HEARING can be broadly translated as a deaf person who chooses "to think and act like a hearing person" (Padden and Humphries 1988, 53). An initial glance at THINK-HEARING could mislead the culturally unacquainted who seek to analyze it. Being articulated at the forehead, the sign could conceivably refer to mental characteristics that usually denote positive values (i.e., intelligence, higher mental aptitude). However, the highlighted feature—speaking—represents an attribute that is not valued within the Deaf culture. Years of unwanted speech training by persons usually woefully ignorant of the deleterious effect of this imposed training have resulted in a large number of deaf people who do not appreciate speech.

Other negative associations are linked with THINK-HEARING, including: (1) because ASL is communicated via a gestural/visual modality, speaking, which is irrelevant, is not valued in the Deaf culture; (2) when an attempt is made to simultaneously use ASL and spoken English, the syntactic structures of the two languages

SPEAK   THINK-HEARING

Figure 15. Cumulative metaphtonymy

(and modalities) clash; (3) there is the belief that someone who does not cherish ASL above English is suspect in many culturally driven ways. The negative label can be attached to any deaf or hard of hearing person, even those who may actually value the use of both ASL and English.[14] This sign has complex negative, "hearing" connotations based on educational, political, and societal constraints that hearing people have traditionally imposed upon the Deaf community.

Etymologically, the word derives from a sign that is often glossed as SPEAK or SAY (see fig. 15). It is articulated at the mouth, with tiny circular movements that visually indicate the flow of speech from the person who is talking. The sign SPEAK is metonymic because the circling movements stand for the warm breath emanating from the speaker's mouth. The exhaled air is metonymically extended to stand for the speech produced by the person. Speech is then viewed as a metonym for the language spoken. In a semantically extended sense, SPEAK has also come to represent, and is often glossed as, HEARING-PERSON. In fact, it is unclear whether SPEAK and HEARING-PERSON are not presently two distinct lexical items with the same form, which had one source in an earlier period of the language.[15] Thus, the circling movements that represent speech are an example of synecdoche, where a part (the act of speaking) stands for the whole (the hearing person doing the speaking). In turn, another metonym is derived when the word representing the hearing person is also used to represent the thoughts and culture of such a person. Recall that metonymy allows referential functioning, with the aspect picked out to *stand for* something becoming the focus of the

---

14. Padden and Humphries (1988, 53-54) consider this labeling to be a "trendier accusation" since older members of the community are unfamiliar with issues involving the political implications of the kind of signing one uses. The younger generation is more aware of the "sophistication with sign structure," and the fact that some signers "use among themselves invented sign vocabulary developed for teaching English to deaf children," and find this unacceptable.

15. I would like to acknowledge an unidentified reviewer for noting this point.

frame. In this case, it is not the auditory acuity of the hearing person that is cognitively highlighted; it is the act of speaking that acquires the focus.

When the sign is placed at a different location, multiple metonyms are further derived. It becomes what Goossens (1990, 338) calls *cumulative metaphtonymy*—a metaphor derived from metonymy. The sign is moved from the mouth area to the forehead. By virtue of this simple change in location, HEARING-PERSON (SPEAK) becomes THINK-HEARING (see fig. 15). The forehead is a metonym for the brain, which can serve as an ontological metaphor for a container of thought processes. When these thought processes are considered to be a hearing person's thought processes (THINK-HEARING), there is a cognitive invitation to compare the deaf person's thought processes with the thought processes of the hearing person. The metonymic expression THINK-HEARING takes on metaphoric mapping. The sign no longer refers only to the voice production of the speech mechanism, to its additional metonymic extension, a hearing person, or even to the extended metonym for the culture and values of hearing people. By virtue of placement at the location of thought processing, the sign SPEAK, when referring to a deaf individual, assumes mappings from the speech domain and speech related cultural values. These values of speech map onto the target domain of a deaf person's thoughts. The word metaphorically takes on the instantiation of bigotry.

SPEAK, which is in the speech domain, thus comes to refer to a person who has at least some degree of hearing loss, who "thinks like a hearing person," accepts speech and speech-related signing, values the ways of the hearing world, rejects ASL, and so forth. In other words, these deaf and hard of hearing people choose "to embrace uncritically the ideology of others" (Padden and Humphries 1988, 53). Rutherford explains that the word is used as "a derogatory identification" of people with hearing loss who use English, and is "directly analogous to calling a black person an 'Oreo'" (1989, 79). This ideology maps onto the SPEAK sign through a subtle metonymic extension once again. The image schema of "spoken language values" within a hearing person's mind is mapped onto the SPEAK sign by virtue of its placement at the forehead—where thoughts are commonly considered to reside. Because this sign, when placed at the forehead, typically is used to designate a person who has a hearing loss, and because "spoken language values" are universally negatively viewed in the Deaf culture, the labeling as a whole carries powerful cultural force. The cumulative metaphtonymic expression clearly validates the mental interaction of cognitive structures found in the language of ASL and is one more example of the complex interaction of metonymy and metaphor.

Both simile and metonymy are irrevocably intertwined with metaphor throughout the ASL lexicon. John-Steiner recognizes this alliance: "The power of visual thinking is that it illuminates and makes manifest this ability to conceptualize our experiences as structures in motion, as relationships" (1985, 83).

5

METAPHORICAL MAPPING IN AMERICAN SIGN LANGUAGE

The linguistic picture that ASL presents to the world is molded in part by the metaphorical mapping of concepts onto actual hand-shape formations and articulations. The hands reveal relationships of form, movement, and location through mental concepts that are motivated by the daily experiences of its language users.

Spatial concepts emerge from our physical interaction with the environment. In spoken English, this results in the prevalent use of spatial terms such as up-down, front-back, in-out, near-far, and so forth, which correspond to everyday bodily functioning. The semantic groundings of these terms motivate metaphorical mapping of spatial concepts into the expressions of the spoken language.

Spatial grounding of meaning can also be immediately recognized in ASL. In the up-down category, the metaphorical mapping of "upness"—or more specifically, an orientational metaphor GOOD IS UP—occurs in signs such as HAPPY, RICH, IMPROVE, POSITIVE, SUCCESS, INVENT, WIN, EXCITE, PROMOTION, and SMILE, as well as many others (see fig. 16). Lakoff and Johnson document that the **good is up** metaphor is used extensively in English; for example, "Everything's coming *up* roses!" "Things are looking *up*," and "They do *high*-quality work" (1980, 16–19). The metaphor occurs pervasively in ASL, too. The handshapes and initial locations for these signs differ, although each one involves an obvious upward motion. Further, although some of the signs in figure 16 are executed with a degree of upward movement, none is taken to mean "up" literally. The positive value of "goodness" maps onto the meaning of the lexical item through the upward movement of the sign itself, becoming a metaphorical reference. Conversely, a downward movement may indicate a lack of positive values in the meaning of the signs: POOR, SAD, KILL, DECREASE, LOSE, FAIL, CAN'T, CHEAT, CRY, or DENY (see fig. 16).

Wilbur (1987) shows that this up-down spatialization motivates metaphorical mapping, but that palm orientation has an influence as well. For example, the ASL signs GOOD and BAD both move downward. However, orientation of the palm differentiates the two signs: GOOD is made with the palm up, and BAD is made with the palm down. A second variation can be seen in alternatives such as LIKE/DON'T LIKE, or WANT/DON'T WANT. While the positive forms of

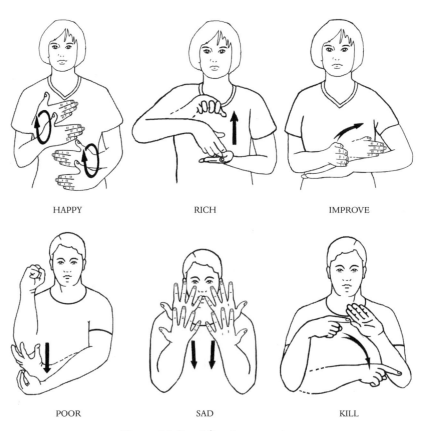

Figure 16. Spatialization mapping

these pairs are not necessarily motivated by upward movements, the negative forms use marking in which movement is away from the origin of the sign, with an additional downward movement possible. In these marked cases, "down is negative," and the downward movement metaphorically maps negation onto the unmarked signs (1987, 174):

"up is unmarked" [positive]	"down is negative"
APPEAR	DISAPPEAR
WANT	DON'T-WANT
HAVE	DON'T-HAVE
KNOW	DON'T-KNOW
LIKE	DON'T-LIKE
WITH	WITHOUT

Lakoff and Johnson (1980, 7–13) have shown that our conceptual system is systematic and motivated, not unstructured and accidental. Metaphors express coherent and systematic relationships between concepts. For example, they have found that time is metaphorically conceptualized in terms of space in English. The mapping is motivated by unidirectionality and linearity, and is found in many coherent mappings of space and time (e.g., *around* ten o'clock, *in* an hour, *at* dawn, *before* midnight).

In ASL, information regarding time can be expressed in relation to what is known as the *time line*. One indicator of this metaphorical concept of time is the direction of the movement along the time line, with each time sign running along an imaginary line through the body. The signer's body represents present time, and areas in the front and back of the body represent future and past, respectively. Time signs such as NOW, WILL, and ONE-DAY-PAST have relative locations on the time line that agree with their temporal meanings, although the relative locations are not to scale. For example, the spatial stations for LONG-LONG-AGO and PAST are relatively close, considering the temporal distance possible between the two terms. ASL represents time as a perceptual experience in terms of spatial paths and temporal unidirectionality. The ASL time line enables time to be perceived as running from past (back) to future (front). The front and the back of a human body corresponds to the body's daily movement patterns of moving ahead (into the future) or stepping back (into the past).

English expands the use of spatial unidirectionality through the metaphors **life is a journey** (e.g., "I'm at a crossroads"; "She needs a new direction in life") and **love is a journey** (e.g., "Look how far we've come"; "This marriage is at a dead end") (Lakoff and Johnson 1980). In ASL, the metaphor THOUGHT IS A JOURNEY maps event structures onto time structures.

Sweetser (1992a) claims that the mind-as-body metaphor suggests that reasoning, which may be the most purposeful mode of thought, can be viewed metaphorically as an activity that exhibits spatial interaction (e.g., "We reason *from* premises *to* conclusions, which we eventually *reach* or *arrive at*") (1992a, 716). In ASL, thought structures map onto time structures, thus following the unidirectionality of the time line. In an English conversation the expression **Do you follow me?** is seen as a joint thought-journey metaphor, an instantiation of **speech exchange is a shared journey** (Sweetser 1992a). The English speaker controls the direction of the mental journey, the conversation.

ASL thought-events follow some, but not all, of the experiential instantiations of the English metaphor **speech exchange is a shared journey.** ASL does not expect thought to be directed solely by the speaker, with the conversational partner being guided in common thought processes along the path of shared discourse. In fact, in many ways, the partner is as critical a guide during ASL discourse as the speaker. Perhaps this is due to the fact that ongoing mutual comprehension and feedback is imperative for appropriate ASL discourse to occur.

English speakers travel metaphorically from location to location throughout a shared journey (e.g., "Are you lost?" "I'm right with you." "Can you follow that?") (Sweetser 1992a, 716). Conversely, if an ASL speaker asks others if they are "lost," the meaning associated with the sign LOST is generally understood as a physical orientation, rather than a metaphorical one.[1] Also, if a deaf person asks someone, "Are you with me?" the question has a literal meaning and does not lend itself to the thought and communication patterns instantiated by **speech exchange is a shared journey**. However, the metaphor **thought is a journey**, especially where reasoning is concerned, is realized in the following ASL signs OFF-THE-SUBJECT, BACK-UP, LEAP-AHEAD.

A unidirectional path in space becomes an anchor for signs connected to reasoning, as exemplified in OFF-THE-SUBJECT: "He is obviously off-track." The index finger makes a dramatic 90-degree shift from a front-moving path to either side of the time line, or "path of reason," when this sign is produced. Another sign, BACK-UP, refers to going back to the beginning, with the two index fingers stepping backwards in circles along the time line path. This unidirectional path is consistent with the metaphor of a logical thought having a beginning and an end. The speaker is being urged to go back to the beginning—at the initial point of logic—to begin explaining again. An ASL speaker can also admonish someone to avoid jumping to conclusions. The sign LEAP-AHEAD makes use of the Frozen V classifier discussed later in this chapter (see section on the interaction of metaphor and metonymy) and iconically appears as though a thought structure is jumping forward on two legs.

All three of the signs (OFF-THE-SUBJECT, BACK-UP, LEAP-AHEAD) relate to points along the time line. However, it is not time that is most salient in these metaphors; it is space. THOUGHT IS A JOURNEY is consistent with MENTAL STATES ARE LOCATIONS. These two metaphors, and other coherently related time, space, and thought metaphors, generate conventional metaphorical expressions in ASL. Lexical items such as *follow, with,* and *lost,* which normally

---

1. ASL speakers can, however, assert that they are "lost" if they do not comprehend a speaker's message. Further research is needed to determine whether the language allows the speaker to *ask* this question without the accompanying epistemic metaphor described later in this chapter, IDEAS NOT FULLY IN EXISTENCE ARE BENT.

occur in the **speech exchange is a shared journey** metaphor in English, are not pervasively found in ASL.

The ASL examples described in this section illustrate structured relationships between time and space that are dependent upon human experience and culturally grounded concepts in our environment. Our everyday interaction with the physical environment and members of our cultural group motivates systematic aspects of the mind. Time and space obviously play important roles in characterizing linguistic form in ASL. Even a perfunctory analysis of this temporal-spatial phenomenon indicates regularities coherent with metaphors in our conceptual system and demonstrates that the experiential grounding discussed in chapter 1 seems to be at least as prevalent in ASL as in spoken languages. However, the mappings that occur in ASL are not always identical to the mappings found in English.

Categorization of IDEAS ARE OBJECTS

Categorization is not a simple concept, whether in the realm of cognitive linguistics or metaphors in ASL. Berlin, following Rosch's (1973) findings on categorization, found that the psychologically most basic level was in the middle of the taxonomic hierarchies (cited in Lakoff 1987b, 46):

Superordinate:	animal	furniture
Basic Level:	dog	chair
Subordinate:	retriever	rocker

This taxonomy reflects the hierarchy found in the organization of conceptual levels. At the basic level things are usually correlated with functions, and those things usually determine the way an object is perceived. We interact with things through their parts; therefore, our knowledge is structured via interaction with physical object categories. At the basic level, as opposed to the superordinate level, we perceive shape as a "single mental image" (Lakoff 1987b, 47), based on our common interaction with a familiar object.

The superordinate level is more abstract. Categories at this level cannot be characterized by common visual images or motor actions of the body. For example, there are no mental images of furniture without concrete images of basic-level pieces of furniture—a chair, a table, a bed. At the superordinate level, whether in English or in ASL, the metaphor **mind is a body moving in space** is not an "imaginable" category. We do not mentally picture a single visual image to represent this metaphor. In order to understand it, we must shift to the basic-level category where we can mentally "flesh it out" in terms of physical activity. At this level we can imagine a body or an object journeying through space.

The subordinate level houses metaphors with a more elaborate representation of the physical source domain. For example, the richer the image evoked at this level, the more subordinate the metaphor. A specific mental image can be more readily mapped onto a concept at this level; here we find our "novel" and imaginative metaphorical expressions.

The general metaphorical class **ideas are objects** is found at the superordinate level of categorization. It is difficult to conceive of the objects in this class without first projecting a shape or form onto the mental conceptualization. We will see that at the basic level ideas generated from this metaphor can be conceived of with manageable parts, animate or inanimate. However, it can also be argued that the metaphor can be represented at *the upper level* of the basic-level category, since objects appear to interact on a physical level with us—although we must map a shape or schema onto the object before being able to conceive of it.

The cline between the higher (superordinate) level and the lower (subordinate) level of categories is gradual and often relative. There are no clear distinctions separating each level, nor are the distinctions necessary in order to understand the metaphor. It may even be possible that the basic level is structured into two (or more) complex levels within a level.

The Metaphor: **The Mind Is a Container**

Our conceptual system is so fundamentally metaphorical, and spatialization is such an inherent part of the way we conceptualize

the basic-level metaphor **the mind is a container** can
.d by the reader without effort. Not only do readers of
ıceptualize this metaphor, but Jakel has documented the
conta...._ netaphor in the Danish, Hebrew, Indonesian, Japanese,
Malayalam, Swahili, Tamil, and Turkish languages (1993). The following metaphorical examples require unconscious conceptualization of a mental container in order to comprehend the functioning
of many of the ASL classifier morphemes documented in this
chapter.

Lindner's (1981) description of over six hundred verbs containing
the particle *out* (e.g., spread out, watch out, time out) documented
the huge number of terms in the English lexicon that deal with the
extended concept of an interior and an exterior. The physical body
itself is constrained by its skin and represents the prototypical
human conception of in-ness and out-ness. People unconsciously
relate to the world around them as entities bounded by territorial
surfaces. Lindner's intensive examination of the English word *out*
highlighted an enormous number of activities that can be subsequently conceptualized in terms of a container schema. Sweetser
elaborates, "We regularly use the vocabulary of our body's physical
center-periphery and container structure to refer to the structure of
our psychological, moral, intellectual abstract selves" (1992b, 6).
The container schema is prevalent in ASL also, as shown in the
analysis below.

Wilbur (1987, 177) found that consultants made use of the C
handshape at the front of the forehead to demonstrate that the
mind could be visualized as a "full" container, a container with so
much experience and knowledge that the forehead conceptually expands beyond its original shape. The handshape could also collapse,
thereby representing a mind that "suffers a momentary lapse in
thought or an incomplete understanding of a topic" (177). One
consultant created a sign by using his left hand with the C classifier
at his forehead, and the right hand making the movement of an
Open 8 handshape (a handshape normally signed on the back of the
hand to mean "empty") inside the C classifier of the left hand. This

illustrated that the container, the mind, was devoid of any thoughts or knowledge.

A similar metaphor was found in my data corpus. **The mind is a container** metaphor is vividly demonstrated in the sign KNOWL-EDGEABLE (see fig. 17). The consultant showed the amount of knowledge that a native Deaf person should have about his own language by signing a conceptual container that bulged out at the forehead, holding a wealth of information about ASL. He ended by proclaiming that even people with a tremendous amount of practical knowledge might not know the grammatical rules of their own language.

The container metaphor in ASL, however, can be more powerful than a simple ontological metaphor that denotes an abstract entity. There are underlying metaphorical mappings that convey abstract connections within the interior of the container. Image schema patterns found in the internal structure of the container in **the mind is a container** metaphor expand and constrain its semantic functions. These image schemas are the same as those found in English: CONTAINER, SOURCE-PATH-GOAL, LINK, PART-WHOLE, CENTER-PERIPHERY, UP-DOWN, FRONT-BACK (Lakoff 1987b, 282–83).

Figure 17. KNOWLEDGEABLE

An organism that has never experienced gravity or self-propulsion might not conceive of movements perpendicular to the earth's crust in the same way that an organism subjected to gravity and self-propulsion does.[2] The human body is aware of the consequences of its interactions with the world. For example, the body runs toward what is ahead of it, not what is behind it. The body is usually able to negotiate the pathway in front more effectively than the path behind. Turner (1991, 69) considers the front-back differentiation to be a consequence of interactions that a typical human body will have with the world around it. Although environmental interactions are generally the same in all directions, the functional constraints built into our bodies by the fact that we have a front and a back contribute to our conceptualization of front-back differentiation.

In English, front-back differentiation contributes to linguistic expressions that reflect this fundamental aspect of interaction with the world (e.g., "It's in the back of my mind somewhere"). ASL also distinguishes the front from the back, creating rich semantic expressions. The brain is an organ that regulates human thought and body functioning. Most of the consultants made reference to the physical structure of the brain to some extent, indicating that they were aware of hemisphere dominance and so forth. Nevertheless, all ASL consultants systematically used the site near the center or off-center from the forehead as the area for the placement of "thinking" signs. This folk model of where the seat of thinking takes place in ASL is reminiscent of other folk models, such as our model for conceptualizing wolves. People may know that wolves are shy and reticent, usually anxious to avoid human contact. However, the folk model of a wolf is different—

---

2. Mark Turner (1991, 38-39) recognizes the unconscious aspect of thought processing that is suffused with awareness of our bodies: "up and down, forward and back, right and left, continuity and discreteness, linearity, circularity, paths, progress, boundaries, contact, interiors and exteriors, centers, penetration, covering, occlusion, discovery, pain, and the great rest of the basic conceptual apparatus we bring to bear in making what is usually automatic and unconscious sense of our worlds."

beware the ferocity of the dangerous beast. Deaf people know that the brain's activities are specialized; nevertheless, they systematically pattern the area of the forehead as being responsible for conscious thinking when using ASL, as exemplified by signs such as REMEMBER, SENILE, UNDERSTAND, MEMORIZE, LEARNED-LESSON-NEVER-AGAIN, FORGET, THINK, STUPID, CRAZY, SMART, BRILLIANT, GENIUS, MULL-OVER, WONDER, MIND-BLANK, ETCH-ON-MIND, INVENT, MAKE-UP, IMAGINE, IDEA, CONCEPT, PEA-BRAIN, IGNORANT, KNOW-NOTHING, OPINION, WISE, SUSPICIOUS, PUZZLE, KNOW, KNOWLEDGE, DON'T KNOW, OPEN-MINDED, THEORY and HYPOTHESIS.[3]

The signs in the above paragraph are not conventionally accepted at the "unconscious thinking" area found at the far back side of the head. This is the area that (1) metaphorically hides information from other speakers, or (2) is truly inaccessible to the signer under normal thought processing, or (3) has stored knowledge, perhaps gained through years of experience. The language model in figure 18 is demonstrating the sign KNOWLEDGE-STORE. Instead of placing the dominant hand at the forehead, as when signing KNOW, he places it toward the back of his head, indicating that knowledge derived from great experience was stored in that particular part of the brain.

One consultant created a joke to relate how *REMEMBER might be used (see fig. 19). He explained that after telling a friend to be sure to REMEMBER (consciously), he could also be told to *REMEMBER (unconsciously), encouraging the friend to "cover all bases," so to speak. The consultant acknowledged that while the friend would probably understand the meaning of the unconventional sign, there is a chance that he might feel slightly insulted since the insinuation would be that his conscious memory was not sufficient to handle what has to be remembered.

Spatial orientations within ontological container metaphors need to be explored further in ASL. How native signers categorize

---

3. My thanks to Bonnie Rudy for helping to create this list of conscious thinking signs.

Figure 18. KNOWLEDGE-STORE

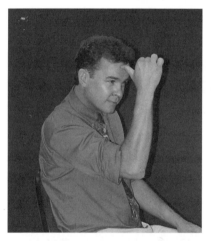

REMEMBER (consciously) *REMEMBER (unconsciously)

Figure 19. Spatial orientations

experiences may be manifested in the way the mind conceives of its own territoriality. For example, even the conventional sign KNOW has not yet been sufficiently explored by linguists. Lakoff and Johnson quotes Taub's work on conceptual metaphors, saying that "the sign meaning *know* has the dominant forefinger moving to the forehead, tracing the path of a piece of knowledge coming into the head" (1999, 86). This is similar to the description proposed by Gee and Kegl in which the G classifier represents a "line of thought" that projects thoughts inward to the mind (1982, 196).

There is another way to conceptualize what is taking place when a person "knows" something. The physical forms of KNOW are either similar or identical (depending on which variant of KNOW is specified) to the handshapes for MY, OWN, existential HAVE, and POSSESS. This changes the metaphor to a form of territorial possession that specifies where the knowledge is and who possesses it, rather than a stream of knowledge flowing through a conduit pipe to a location. The etymology of KNOW suggests that the old ASL INFORM was articulated first with the sign KNOW, then with both vertical handshapes moving downward and outward as if giving out knowledge (Higgins 1923, 83). This form would motivate the modern ASL KNOW as information to store in the brain and to own or to disperse. The conduit "lines of thought," representing information flowing outward from the brain, would not be as motivating. This acknowledged etymological path for KNOW suggests that even common, conventional signs in ASL need further investigation.

Basic-Level Mapping: IDEAS ARE OBJECTS SUBJECT TO PHYSICAL FORCE

The conventional ontological metaphor **ideas are objects** is based on our perceptions of physical objects and how they function under certain conditions (Lakoff and Johnson 1980, 1999). In English, structural metaphors such as this one can highlight, downplay, or hide similarities between the perceptions we have about common objects and how we perceive them to be similar to ideas or thoughts (e.g., "That idea is *buried* beneath irrelevant prose"; "Try to *capture* that idea before it flits away"). Searle (1986) recognizes that metaphors are both restrictive and systematic. This constrained patterning is realized in ASL.

English speakers normally use somewhat more fleshed-out versions of the **ideas are objects** metaphor. Similarly, when ASL informants articulate expressions from the same general class of metaphor, they use different classifier handshape morphemes, depending on the similarities between the source and target domains that a particular instantiation is highlighting or hiding. This choice of morphemes is not random; it is systematically patterned. In ASL, the "handle" classifier handshapes (a set of handshapes that indicate the shape of an object and the manner in which the object is manipulated or handled) are used to maintain distinct and systematic referencing. This helps to provide a shared system of principles that allow ASL users to comprehend linguistic variables when discussing sets of unspecified referents. The handle verb stem morphemes provide the systematicity necessary for the patterned restrictions that must underlie certain metaphorical utterances.

McDonald's (1982) work focused on the function of predicate classifier verb stems, especially the way ASL signals the fact that an object is handled or manipulated. She identified eighteen distinct handle classifiers (i.e., handle a flat plane; handle a spherical, flat object; handle a compact transportable object). The prominent semantic function of these classifiers is not necessarily dictated by their shapes, but by the ways in which objects are moved and handled. The semantic function found in certain handle morphemes plays an important role in the analysis of ASL metaphors connected with thoughts and ideas.

IDEAS ARE OBJECTS may be found either in the superordinate category (where ideas have no shapes) or in the upper level of the basic-level category (where ideas have shapes determined by the image schemas mapped onto the ideas). The cline is further complicated with IDEAS ARE OBJECTS SUBJECT TO PHYSICAL FORCE, a fairly superordinate-level category, although it evokes metaphorical expressions that can be categorized at the basic or subordinate levels. Lakoff and Johnson found that there is not always a clear-cut distinction between literal and metaphorical structuring in English (1980, 1999). The catetgorical cline in ASL appears to be just as complicated.

In the IDEAS ARE OBJECTS SUBJECT TO PHYSICAL FORCE metaphor, the hands are often the direct cause of the manipulation in the physical source domain. The size and types of physical objects manipulated by the hands in the activities occurring in the source domain generally correspond with the shape and manipulability of the image schema that is transferred to the target domain. In other words, the image schemas from activities in the source domain influence the phonological selection of the handle morpheme, which is critical to the coherence of referents found in the target domain. The verb stem handshape provides the pattern of shared systematicity that Searle (1986) found to be so vital to the comprehension and communicability of metaphors. The features of a *size and shape specifier*—a classifier—are salient, common, and distinctive; they are familiar to users of ASL. The image schemas of classifiers found in the source domain regularly map onto distinct aspects of the target domain.

The pliability and physical maneuverability of an object is represented in ASL in a constrained fashion by the choice of a particular classifier morpheme that restricts characteristics or patterns of object-manipulation. For example, picking up a small object such as a comic book requires a handshape morpheme different from one used to delicately extract a seed. The literal function of a classifier morpheme replicates itself when used to show the abstract functioning that occurs in target domain conceptualization.

In literal ASL usage, a handle classifier is chosen in part to replicate the appropriate shape and size of the specified object. However, in metaphorical extension, it is often the *function* (e.g., how we use the object) that is primarily relevant, rather than the size and shape attribute of the object. In the following basic-level metaphors dealing with thoughts and ideas, some instances of the size and shape image schema exhibited by a handle morpheme are systematically relegated to a lesser status when mapped onto the target domain. The source domain referent dealing with function can then be underscored. Nevertheless, size is still relevant since the mapping of highlighted referents from the source domain to the target domain often requires discriminating aspects of size and shape. Examples of how handshapes and their physical structures play a prominent role in the conceptualization of ASL metaphors are illustrated in the following paragraphs.

IDEAS ARE OBJECTS TO BE MANIPULATED OR PLACED

Extending from the IDEAS ARE OBJECTS SUBJECT TO PHYSICAL FORCE metaphor (a subcategory of IDEAS ARE OBJECTS), is the basic-level metaphor IDEAS ARE OBJECTS TO BE MANIPULATED OR PLACED (see fig. 20).[4] If ideas are metaphorically understood as objects, they can be moved, placed, manipulated, picked up, co-located, separated, and so on. The morpheme used for the handling of a "thin, flattish, wide object" is appropriate when there is little need for an object to be grasped tightly. This follows the literal manipulation of objects in the real world—where there is little need to worry about a familiar object disappearing from sight, nor is there reason to tightly clutch an object for fear that it will fall from the hands. The handshape chosen to highlight a specific activity depends on the type of manipulation of the object in the source domain. In this case, a Flat O morpheme is used because of the metaphor's function: controlled manipulation of an idea.

The verb stem shown in figure 20 would not motivate a conceptualization of a large, rectangular box-type object. That particular handle morpheme, Flat O, allows the manipulation of a flat, thin object such as a sheet of paper or a thin pamphlet. Lifting up a heavy box with this handshape would be a difficult manual task. This indicates that the iconic representation of the object (size or shape) to be moved or manipulated is still an important feature to be considered. However, with the basic-level metaphor IDEAS ARE OBJECTS TO BE MANIPULATED OR PLACED, the key semantic referent is the *function*—manipulation—rather than the shape of the object being held.[5]

When predicate verb stem morphemes are used literally as size and shape specifiers, the size and shape of an object is emphasized. For example, when using this classifier morpheme literally, common, thin, flat objects are moved or reorganized in a deliberate

---

4. This study glosses "ideas" alternatively as "thoughts."

5. Ideas can be metaphorically conceptualized as "thin, flat objects" at the subordinate level of categorization also (see fig. 34a–h).

METAPHORICAL MAPPING IN ASL

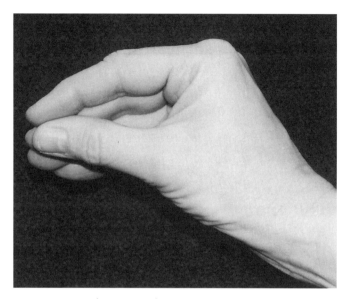

Figure 20. Flat O morpheme: IDEAS ARE OBJECTS TO BE
MANIPULATED OR PLACED

manner. The image schemas of the Flat O morpheme found in the source domain—controlled movement and manipulation by the handler, familiarity of the object, and deliberate placement—readily map onto the target domain of abstract ideas being moved. Semantic referents that deal with the manipulated and controlled movement of the morpheme are mapped.

When an idea is being moved around in deliberation or is placed in co-location with other ideas, the Flat O classifier can be used to indicate the metaphorical manipulation of the idea. Part of the image schema dealing with size may be relevant, however, since the chosen morpheme is contingent upon the physical characteristics of the source domain object being handled. A tiny piece of lint would not require the neuromuscular effort of four fingertips and a thumb in order to be picked up. In fact, such a choice would be a physical hindrance. By the same reasoning, an inappropriately selected handshape for handling objects would not coherently map onto the target domain of ideas that *do* require controlled deliberations of movement.

It must be emphasized that this study does not exclude the value and importance of physical characteristics evoked by classifier hand-shapes. Rather, it notes that function can be a predominant aspect of object handling involved in some of the basic metaphorical mappings that deal with ideas and thoughts. The Flat O morpheme used in figure 20 demonstrates this highlighting of metaphorical manipulation.

Recall from chapter 4 (see fig. 10) the simile segment translated as: *"We see the same thing in a cartoon that has images of ideas inside the bubble—flashing about like glistening lights and popping sparklers—until the thoughts are placed exactly the way the mind wishes them to be, arranged just so, with all thoughts coherent and whole"* (glossed as PICTURE, C-A-R-T-O-O-N, LIKE, SPARKLE, STARS, SMOKE, TOUCH-UP, MOVE$_1$, MOVE$_2$, NICE, PERFECT). In figure 21, the picture shows the ideas and thoughts found within the simile segment being *controlled and manipulated*. They are being shifted around and placed into positions with other ideas. Nothing within the content of the signed discourse indicates that detailed shape has been mapped onto the ideas. The image schema transferred from the source domain is an activity of *controlled* physical movement in which a person does not have to worry about an object getting away or falling from one's grasp. The image schema also maps vague physical characteristics evoked by the classifier handshape form. However, the critical semantic component found in the target domain of the metaphor is the controlled manipulation of the ideas and thoughts being moved around.

Another example emphasizes function over physical size and shape, using the Flat O verb stem morpheme (see fig. 22a). The consultant demonstrated how ideas could be placed at the back of the head, which was described as an area of unconscious thinking. At no point in the discourse was reference made to the shape or size of the idea being moved to that location. The idea involved seemed to be a "generic" thought without any descriptive embellishment of characteristics or physical form (i.e., not *a lovely little idea*). The Flat O handshape served as a vehicle for metaphorically transporting the generic thought into the unconscious area of the brain. The image schemas of the use and function of this handshape from the

METAPHORICAL MAPPING IN ASL

MOVE₁ and MOVE₂

Figure 21. Manipulation of thoughts

source domain (controlled movement and manipulation, familiarity of the object, deliberate placement) map onto the target domain of placement of an abstract thought in a specific location. Metaphorical mapping is achieved through the use of an appropriate morpheme that allows the necessary constrained referents to be unidirectionally mapped. Because little reference is made to the size and shape of the generic thought, this sign could conceivably fit within Quadrant #3 of table 2 in chapter 4, (if loose iconic standards were applied). Thus, the minus iconic, plus metaphorical criterion applies.

In contrast, one sign taken from the data, COCHLEAR-IMPLANT-DEVICE, shows a strong similarity between the handshape used for the Flat O handle classifier and an iconic handshape used to designate that a cochlear implant device has been surgically implanted behind the ear. The location of the auditory device is close to the unconsciousness site of mental thought processing used in KNOWLEDGE-STORE (see fig. 18). Because the discourse deals only with the literal manipulation of an object, no conceptual domains were crossed. This sign falls into Quadrant #2 in the relationship between iconicity and metaphoricity. In this case, the size, shape, and location are

PUT-KNOWLEDGE (into "unconscious thinking" area)   COCHLEAR-IMPLANT-DEVICE

Figure 22. Metaphorical and literal classifiers

equally critical components to the comprehension of the sign COCHLEAR-IMPLANT-DEVICE. No metaphorical mapping takes place.

Consultants indicate that an idea can be moved metaphorically to the top or to the bottom of a list, or placed on another list altogether. Ideas can also be arranged and straightened up (as in fig. 21). In each instance, the Flat O classifier moves the ideas in some orderly fashion, revealing that referents from source domain activities in which the function of intention and controlled manipulation—rather than the shape attribute—map onto the target domain conceptualization. Through the use of this morpheme, as much schematic structure of the source domain is mapped as is consistent with the intended preservation of the target domain. Thus, the Invariance Hypothesis (Brugman 1990; Lakoff 1990; Lakoff and Turner 1989; Turner 1990, 1991) finds support from the ASL data.

IDEAS ARE OBJECTS TO BE GRASPED

We have already seen in chapter 4 how a single handshape—the container classifier—is both iconic and metaphoric. In the section above, the Flat O handle classifier is also found in both iconic and metaphoric signs in ASL. Another handshape with possible simulta-

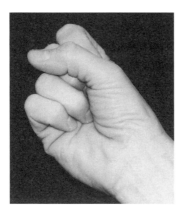

Figure 23. A$_s$ morpheme: IDEAS ARE OBJECTS TO BE GRASPED

neous or alternating dual iconic and metaphoric representation is the fully closed A$_s$ (fist) handshape found in IDEAS ARE OBJECTS TO BE GRASPED (see fig. 23).[6] In ASL discourse, this morpheme can be used when reaching out to grab objects by closing the fingers and thumb into a fist, as in "Ryan scooped up the jewels with one hand." One can easily visualize a fistful of sparkling jewels dangling from between the boy's clutched fingers. The A$_s$ classifier would be represented in Quadrant #2 in this instance.

The same classifier is used for a type of handling that occurs when one wants to "take" a person to another place, such as "I will take Grandmother with me." Although grabbing Grandmother is not the most gentle image imaginable, this sign is typically used in ASL to grab or place a person. The A$_s$ classifier in this case is still iconic. The fist is used to conceptualize the intention of holding on to a material substance—a person—just as it clutched the jewels in the previous illustration. The iconic concepts involved concern animate and inanimate, but nevertheless physical, objects. The A$_s$ classifier occurs when something is being contained in the hands or hung on to tightly.

---

6. See Anthony Moy's (1990) work on the psycholinguistic approach to categorizing handshape in ASL. The A$_s$ allophone stands for the S handshape in the manual alphabet.

This A_s classifier also can be used metaphorically. The same fist classifier is involved, but instead of holding onto a person or some other physical substance, the signer "holds onto" abstract ideas, thoughts, or memories (in English: "Hang on to that idea!"). This particular handshape is used when mapping the grasping of an object in such a way that it cannot escape, onto the cognitive process of permanently holding on to an idea, thought, or memory. In the source domain, using a classifier of this physical configuration entails more than the size or shape of an enclosed object.

This handshape function deals with possession and retention of an object, regardless of how large or small that object may be or whether the object is concrete or abstract. A physical item does not have to be tiny enough to fit within the palm of the clinched fist. The image schema of *custody*, without respect to size, is mapped onto the target domain. In this way, even the accumulated ideas or memories of a lifetime can be metaphorically held in one tight-fisted hand. It is not the image schema of the object's size that is mapped onto the target domain. The constraining guardianship of an abstract thought is highlighted when this basic-level metaphor is realized through the use of the A_s morpheme. The concept conveyed by the handshape is metaphorical, although the morpheme maintains the mapping of an iconic layer by virtue of the shape of its enclosed grip.

Several different metaphors blend to create the coherent basic-level metaphorical expression seen in figure 24. The superordinate-level metaphor IDEAS ARE OBJECTS allows the IDEAS ARE OBJECTS SUBJECT TO PHYSICAL FORCE metaphor to be instantiated by the use of the basic-level morpheme, the A_s classifier. The consultant explained that he had traveled the world collecting folklore in an attempt to create a record of the humor, jokes, and visual memorabilia that circulate among deaf people. He indicated that he had been acquiring clever ideas that he saw in the Deaf community, storing into his mind hundreds of delightful stories and bits of "play on hands" that might someday fade from the scene if no one recorded them. His intention was to eventually gather them from his mind and place them in a historical document of folklore.

Figure 24. "Pool-ideas-into-book"

The first picture in figure 24 shows the two A_s morphemes that are "holding on to" all of the stored folklore. The collected stories, jokes, puns, and humorous tales are locked tight within the two fists at the forehead. They have been saved for years, awaiting the time for release, as depicted in the second picture. The basic-level metaphor IDEAS ARE OBJECTS TO BE GRASPED, created through the use of the A_s morpheme, now evokes two other elements in Reddy's (1979) conduit metaphor COMMUNICATION IS SENDING and LINGUISTIC EXPRESSIONS ARE CONTAINERS. The analysis that began on just one A_s morpheme now reveals several other metaphors being evoked almost simultaneously.

In the second picture, the mental memoranda are thrown from the forehead area, representing the consultant's decision to release the hundreds of memories from his possession. The ideas are not flung out into the surrounding area where people who happen to be standing around can have access to them. They are flung into the space immediately in front of himself—downward toward his lap area—in the place where a book might be written or held. The ideas are tossed onto a specific location, ready to be packaged into a linguistic "container," a book. All the collected material that was in the consultant's mental control will now be made available to posterity via transfer to the printed page.

Thus, this common source domain activity of gripping tightly to a physical object and tossing it precisely into a container, as when someone tosses a scrap of paper into a trash can, can map onto a target domain in a linguistically rich way. Regardless of the weak isomorphic mapping of size and shape, the primary intent of the A_s morpheme deals with the function of the grasping gesture when used metaphorically. Thoughts can be held in a bondagelike fist without possibility of escape. No seepage of ideas will take place if the function coherent with this particular classifier is maintained. This function is preserved by virtue of the use of the appropriate morpheme—the A_s classifier.

IDEAS ARE OBJECTS TO BE CAREFULLY DISCRIMINATED/SELECTED

When an idea is (metaphorically) carefully discriminated from other ideas and picked up or extracted from the brain, the F classifier (see fig. 25) can be used.[7] The highlighted semantic function is "careful discriminating selection from among a host of possible alternatives."[8] Once again, it is not the emphasis on a "small, tiny object" that is critical to the understanding of this metaphor. The semantics of this morpheme comes from the particular function of selecting an object in a discriminating manner.

When the F classifier is used, one clearly realizes that a huge, box-sized idea is not being removed from the brain. In the source domain, everyday activities do not make use of these delicate fingertips to lift solid, cumbersome objects. Tiny items that are physically lightweight are typically picked up by pinching together the index finger and thumb. Also, some items would fall if a person

---

7. Hand configuration primes have subprime values. Users of ASL will note that the F classifier discussed in this section is a configuration used for signs such as VOTE or TEA, as opposed to the similar handshape for the signs DIPLOMA or COIN.

8. I am grateful to Betsy McDonald for offering this description of the F classifier usage.

METAPHORICAL MAPPING IN ASL

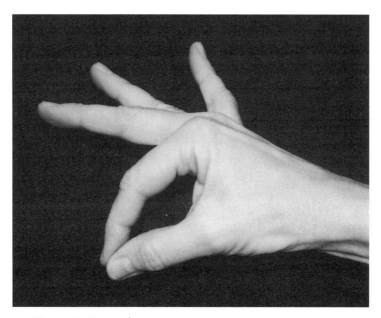

Figure 25. F morpheme: IDEAS ARE OBJECTS TO BE CAREFULLY
DISCRIMINATED/SELECTED

tried to (literally) lift a number of objects all at once with the single
F classifier.

When this morpheme occurs metaphorically, we see that the referents of careful selection and limited quantity map onto the target
domain. The source domain of fine, deliberate motor control maps
onto the target domain of a careful selection of thoughts. The literal use of the F classifier in ASL discourse tends to highlight the
size and shape of an object being picked out; metaphorical use
highlights the intentions of the signer, although an obvious quantity constraint remains.

One consultant explained that it is important to bring ideas down
in front of the body where the information can be seen clearly (see
fig. 26). She explained that while it is acceptable to blindly sort
through ideas located at the forehead or top of the head (see fig.
26a), it is better to firmly push them downward (see fig. 26b), so
that the eyes are afforded an opportunity to LOOK-AT the abstract
items in front of the body (see fig. 26c). Then with the assorted

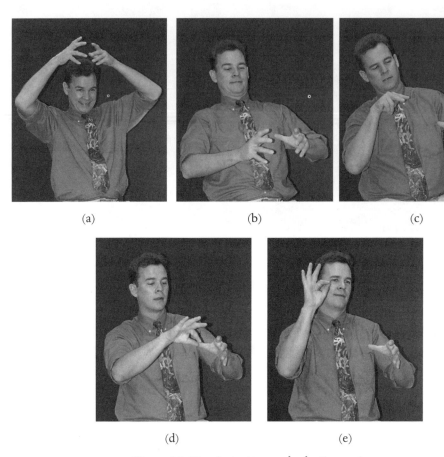

Figure 26. Discriminating and selecting series

thoughts spread out clearly in sight, a discriminating selection of the proper idea can be made (see figs. 26d and 26e).

In addition to highlighting the use of the F classifier morpheme, this example emphasizes the importance of sight to a deaf person. Several times it was stressed that the eyes have to be able to "see" the arrangement of abstract thoughts in order to make a discriminating choice (IDEAS ARE OBJECTS TO BE CAREFULLY SELECTED). The IDEAS ARE OBJECTS and the IDEAS ARE OBJECTS SUBJECT TO PHYSICAL FORCE metaphors were evoked when the consultant explained that the ideas are entities that can be "seen" and that they are objects that can be physically herded and pushed into a position of compliance.

Lakoff and Johnson documented the metaphor **known is down** in English (1980, 20). The experiential basis of reasoning is that an object is easier to grasp and to hold in your hands for examination purposes if it is down on the ground where one can get a fix on it. The task might be impossible if the object were floating up in the air like a maple seed or a feather. The movement evoked in the KNOWN IS DOWN mapping relates to the experiential basis of the IDEAS ARE OBJECTS SUBJECT TO PHYSICAL FORCE described in figure 26b.

Shared Systematicity

The three handle morphemes detailed above (Flat O, A$_s$, and F) were the most commonly found verb stems when consultants discussed movement of abstract ideas, thoughts, and memories at the basic level. Their functions can be summed up as follows:

1. The Flat O morpheme is used if the focus is on the relationship of ideas to one another. Controlled manipulation and placement is considered to be the most important semantic referent.
2. With the A$_s$ classifier, keeping thoughts or memories close at hand becomes salient. The source domain of containment is cognitively mapped so that ideas cannot be taken—until the signer is ready to release them.
3. The F morpheme signals semantic referents associated with discovering a single abstraction following a discriminating process of selection.

These three morphemes play dominant roles in the cognitive processing involved in mapping source domain referents onto target domains. An additional classifier also showed up in the metaphor OBJECTS ARE SUBJECT TO GRAVITY. The morpheme that was used when an idea "leapt" from a brain was a frozen form of the "two-legged" V classifier. An analysis of this conventionalized morpheme can be found in the series of metaphors pictured in figure 34.

The line between literal and metaphorical language may be fuzzy due to the fact that metaphors draw upon literal language in order to form the juxtapositions necessary for target domain mapping (Mac Cormac 1985). The literal use of the verb stem morphemes described above provides evidence in ASL that established categories (classifier sets) can be used to create new ways of understanding abstract thoughts. The metaphorical use of verb stems shows that their basic meaning is not only about size and shape but also about more functional meanings—grasping without escape, selecting, or moving. The verb stems used at this basic level of categorization allow for comparison between physical source domain activities and target domain conceptualizations. They provide the shared restrictions and systematicity that Searle (1986) found to be crucial in order for metaphorical mapping to occur.

The Structural Metaphor: IDEAS IN EXISTENCE ARE STRAIGHT

Attributes are linked to behavior, according to Lakoff and Turner's (1989) commonsense theory of the Nature of Things. In other words, the characteristic behavior of a form of being is a consequence of its characteristic attributes. This theory works to generate a powerful metaphoric conceptualization in ASL. The G classifier [long, thin object], when referred to as thought or idea, visually represents a physical attribute that is pervasively mapped onto aspects of linguistic structure by ASL users.[9]

In the **great chain metaphor** defined by Lakoff and Turner, humans possess higher order attributes (thought and character), but they also have the attributes that animals lower on the hierarchy possess, such as instinctual, biological, structural, and natural physical attributes (1989, 166–213). This **great chain metaphor,** coupled with the **generic is specific metaphor** (understanding a whole category in terms of one), allows humans to link vastly disparate

---

9. The G classifier is also known as a size and shape specifier, such as the CL:1 or the 1→CL (depending on up/down orientation). In this book, slight position changes of the thumb are noted in many of the "long, thin object" signs that are analyzed, but for simplicity, all of the variants will be called the G morpheme or G classifier.

schemas together metaphorically. People are able to link the schemas that characterize knowledge about humans with the schemas that characterize knowledge about physical properties. Thus, the human and the nonhuman can be seen as instances of the same thing through metaphorical mapping of the concrete to the abstract.

Human attributes such as abstract reasoning (i.e., understanding) can be characterized as higher-order attributes. Metaphorical extension of physical and natural behavior allows people to witness daily occurrences of life and see the relationship between a form that is straight and extended with something that is alive and existing. When an animate entity loses its life, it usually undergoes a number of shared physical changes. Whereas there may be initial rigidity upon the death of a living object, its physical composition eventually loses its integrity and sturdiness: it dries up, bends or topples over, crumbles, rots, becomes smaller, and eventually withers away.[10] Conversely, a withered object or deprived being, with the appropriate amount of water, sunshine, and nourishment, may assume an upright posture of vitality or health. All of these characteristics are visible. They represent source domain processes from the environment. Experiential concepts can be metaphorically extended to target domains during abstract thought processing. Thus, ideas, thoughts, or understanding can be metaphorically understood as living things.

In order to comprehend the ASL sign that is glossed into English as an "idea" or a "thought," however, further construal must take place. When metaphorical mapping extends beyond transference from one simple domain to another independent domain, as in the cases of overlapping source and target domains, the conceptual processes become more difficult to analyze (Croft 1991; Fauconnier and Sweetser 1996). Metaphorical mapping in ASL is complicated

---

10. Folk model concepts of material disarray that takes place in the environment recall the second law of thermodynamics, which explains that closed system disorder or entropy increases with time, rather than reverts to cosmological constant (Hawking 1988, 144).

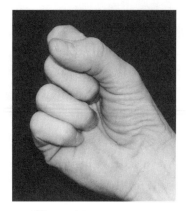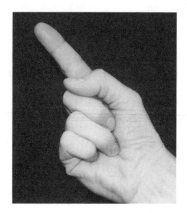

Figure 27. IDEAS IN EXISTENCE ARE STRAIGHT (UNDERSTAND)

by the issue of an actual, physical form—an isomorphic hand-shape—motivating an additional level of iconicity. ASL metaphoric-ity involves a great degree of iconic transferal from the physical source domain to its physical manifestation on the signer's body and this extra level of complexity is well documented in the data.

Metaphoricity is revealed in the G classifier handshape (see second picture in fig. 27). When referencing the presence of abstract thoughts and coherent ideas, this G classifier represents a structural metaphorical mapping system—IDEAS IN EXISTENCE ARE STRAIGHT. This structural metaphor can be found in signs having to do with mental processing in ASL. For example, the G classifier can be used as a "pointer" to indicate *where* in the brain thinking is assumed to be occurring. When the G classifier is located at or near the forehead it is commonly glossed as THINK. Another sign that deals with mental comprehension is UNDERSTAND. The final finger shape [long, thin object] found in UNDERSTAND is itself a simple icon for upright stature. This icon is a metonym for physical life or existence. From this metonymic concept derives a cumulative metaphtonymy (metaphor induced from a metonym).

Although the G classifier handshape can stand for an upright physical object (human, pole), it also evokes a rich structural metaphor by accepting layers of cognitive mapping. Additional layers of metaphorical extension occur within this handshape when it represents a thought, a memory, or the thinking process itself. No temporal distinction has been discerned in the metaphorical extensions and no order will be accorded any of the following mappings although the conduit metaphorical mapping will be discussed first. It may be that the temporal priority of the mappings depend on the highlighted semantic references that come and go as discourse proceeds.

The general conduit metaphor leads us to conceptualize words and ideas as having physical structures (Reddy 1979). The superordinate metaphor **ideas are objects** is a basic component of the conduit metaphor's powerful logic. When IDEAS ARE OBJECTS maps onto the G classifier as the marker of a source domain object, the unflexed finger sets up a metaphorical mapping that allows it to create a semantic fabric of dual domains. An abstract idea can now conceivably be moved or manipulated, flitted through the air, held tightly in the fist, placed on paper, pierced through the skull, mulled over in the brain, etc. The classifier icon now metaphorically represents a state of being, actuality, or existence. Because IDEAS ARE OBJECTS is a superordinate metaphor that maps onto the index finger, however, there is no rich concrete image schema mapped on to the target domain.

When the sign for a thought or an idea undergoes the manipulations just described, it often does not maintain its original shape—long and thin. Depending upon the manipulation (handshape and movement) involved, it changes shape to fit the contortions of the entity surrounding or embodying it. However, if during discourse it is to maintain its citation shape (long and thin), another cognitive mapping is added to the original idea-object mapping. This is a mapping from the image schema of *straightness* taken from the physical source domain. Cienki describes this **straight** image schema and considers it to be prevalent in our environment, in our manipulation of objects, and in our bodily forms and movements (1998, 108).

Examine the sign that is used to reference an idea or a thought (depending on how it is glossed in interpretation). The G classifier itself is not glossed into English as "straight." In other words, if someone lifted the unflexed index finger, other ASL users would not automatically assume that the person was articulating the sign STRAIGHT. They would perceive, however, that the finger itself was physically extended. They could probably assume that the finger iconically represents an object that is also straight (e.g., a cigarette, a log, a pencil).[11] The unflexed finger icon marks *straightness* in that it refers specifically to long, straight objects, even though it is not necessarily a lexical representation for the word glossed as STRAIGHT. This understanding of the image schematic structure of straightness is based on human perceptual experience. Thus, the iconic concept of *straightness* is an attribute of the G classifier also.

Thus far, in keeping with aspects of the Invariance Hypothesis, the schematic structure of the target images have not been violated. The cognitive mappings noted above have preserved the image schematic structure of the sources and are constrained by the skeletal images in our cognition of "objects" and "straightness". The image schemas—which are not necessarily concrete or even visual images—are mapped onto the physical finger. The recurrent patterns of experiences (with objects and with straightness) provide the source domain for understanding the target domain (abstract thoughts) metaphorically.

Another metaphor to map onto the icon is a superordinate one construed by compiling metaphorical entailments from the previously described mappings: IDEAS IN EXISTENCE ARE STRAIGHT. In addition, the metaphor IDEAS ARE OBJECTS and the physical attribute of straightness offer coherence that satisfies our recognition of environmental perceptual interactions and the cognitive operations that goes with these perceived forces. Shared metaphors can lead to cross-metaphorical coherence. This coherence allows whole metaphorical systems to "come out of our clearly delineated and concrete experiences and allow us to construct highly abstract and elaborate concepts" (Lakoff and Johnson 1980, 105).

---

11. In fact, the classifier 1→CL conventionally stands for long, thin objects such as "pencil, rifle, cigarette, closet rod, cannon, log, pole (on its side), hot dog, and needle" (Baker and Cokely 1980, 290).

"When two metaphors successfully satisfy two purposes, then overlaps in the purposes will correspond to overlaps in the metaphors" (97).

The G classifier icon, which now shares several metaphorical extensions (see fig. 28), including the dominant structure IDEAS IN EXISTENCE ARE STRAIGHT, is a *possible* candidate for another metaphorical mapping: ACCURATE IS STRAIGHT. There are indications that this metaphor is evoked in the language and communication realm. The dominant handshape used for TALK and DISCUSSION, as when a deaf person negotiates a raise or talks over a job-related situation with a supervisor (usually a non-deaf person), is the G morpheme. Typically, "straight" information or "straight" talk takes place when this morpheme is used. In situations where the discourse is expected to be accurate and generally free from conversational "asides," the G classifier is noted. To talk or to discuss something involves the use of ideas and thoughts. Consultants were adamant

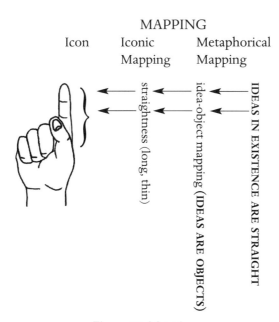

MAPPING

| Icon | Iconic Mapping | Metaphorical Mapping |

straightness (long, thin)

idea-object mapping (IDEAS ARE OBJECTS)

IDEAS IN EXISTENCE ARE STRAIGHT

Figure 28. Mappings

that TALK and DISCUSSION, when using the G classifier, are not articulated with bent index fingers.[12]

Yet further examination of the data reveals that the metaphor ACCURATE IS STRAIGHT—where thoughts and ideas are concerned—does not carry great motivating force, even though it does appear in the language and communication realm. For example, the sign RIGHT is articulated by the use of the two rigidly extended index fingers. These fingers are not representative of any conventional classificatory features (size and shape). In fact, they are not representing any particular physical object. The sign does, nevertheless, indicate a strong meaning of correctness, in the sense that something is accurate. RIGHT's opposite, WRONG, is produced by the use of two extended fingers, the pinkie and the thumb, and is articulated at the chin area, a location known for negation (Frishberg, 1975). This negative semantic field may be enough to have factored out any "straightness" coming from the unflexed thumb and pinkie. This argument, however, is weak. The most convincing argument against the prevalence of the metaphor ACCURATE IS STRAIGHT, is that its opposite does not feature into the analysis coherently. In other words, the *bent* finger does not represent its metaphorical opposite, *INACCURACY IS BENT.

The metaphor IDEAS IN EXISTENCE ARE STRAIGHT is found in the area of abstract thought in ASL. The power of the metaphor is reinforced by its equally pervasive counter-metaphorical mapping, IDEAS NOT FULLY IN EXISTENCE ARE BENT (see below). Thoughts that are coming into conceptual existence take on coherent mapping from experiential grounding in the everyday world about us. We see things blooming, growing, coming into existence, appearing before our eyes. This visual manifestation of living, breathing *existence* maps onto our conceptualization of understanding thoughts and ideas in the abstract domain.

---

12. Both Long (1918) and Higgins (1923) picture the Straight G classifier form for TALK. Diachronic study indicates long-term evidence of straightness in this sign. However, in LSF the sign DISCUTER uses tightly bent index fingers; the French sign is used when discussing a highly controversial or disputed issue or theory.

An idea will suddenly "appear" into consciousness in much the same way that people or objects appear within the limited visual range that makes up a deaf person's receptive environment. Objects pop into the deaf person's peripheral vision. Vehicles, birds, family members, household pets, skateboarders—all appear suddenly and without warning into the visual field of a person who does not hear them approaching. The abrupt manner in which everyday objects project themselves into the awareness of a deaf person's world maps correspondingly onto the target domain of an idea that is suddenly understood.

The metaphors IDEAS IN EXISTENCE ARE STRAIGHT and IDEAS NOT FULLY IN EXISTENCE ARE BENT are vividly exemplified in the minimal pair IDEA-DISAPPEAR/IDEA-DISAPPEAR-PERMANENT (see fig. 29). The G classifier morpheme found in IDEA-DISAPPEAR (not shown) is commonly used when indicating that someone forgot an item or forgot to do something, but with a little luck the memory may return. The dominant G classifier disappears through a "floor" (of consciousness) made of the palm-down fingertips of the nondominant hand during the articulation of DISAPPEAR. If one looks below the floor at the G classifier, however, it can be seen that the index finger is still erect, even though it "disappeared" through the fingertips. The metaphorical concepts mapped onto the erect G classifier finger are still maintained. The idea is still there, and it may possibly reappear at a later time via the IDEAS IN EXISTENCE ARE STRAIGHT metaphor.

On the other hand, IDEA-DISAPPEAR-PERMANENT maps onto the nonexistence found in bent objects seen in the physical source domain. When this idea disappears from view, by bending or flexing the index finger, it is permanently gone. The idea will not be remembered and no attempts are made to recall it. The loss is especially permanent if a variant of the bent finger is used: the A handshape. An idea that goes from being articulated by a straight, erect G classifier morpheme to an A morpheme, is absolutely not going to come back, according to the perception of the consultants. The finger loses all erectness; even the bentness vanishes without a trace into the palm of the hand. Thus, thoughts parallel our daily experi-

Figure 29. IDEA-DISAPPEAR-PERMANENT

ences of watching living things come into being or crumble away—
with the bending or straightening of a finger mirroring life.

Another instantiation of IDEAS IN EXISTENCE ARE STRAIGHT can be
seen in figure 30. A consultant explained that sometimes a teacher
feels that it is necessary to almost "poke" an idea through the skull
of a student who does not catch on to something right away. The
teacher might be required to repeat the explanation over and over
until the idea is finally thrust (metaphorically) into the consciousness of the student. The G classifier evokes IDEAS ARE OBJECTS SUB-
JECT TO FORCE by virtue of its isomorphic resemblance to a nail that
is being hammered through a board. A "long, thin, object" by
virtue of its shape can become an instrument suitable for poking. A
walking cane, a crutch, a kitchen knife, or a closed umbrella are all
more appropriate for piercing a hole than would be a square sugar
cube or a matchbox. In the abstract THINK-PENETRATE, the nondominant hand assumes metonymic dimensions as the "wall of the
brain" that the idea must be projected through. This wall represents
a further metonymic extension for a container, as in the metaphor
THE MIND IS A CONTAINER. The metaphorical referent that is highlighted by the finger icon is the *act of penetration* that occurs when
the index finger breaks through the closed fingertips. This referent
is appropriate since the comprehension that occurs in the target do-

Figure 30. THINK-PENETRATE

main when a person understands a difficult concept is metaphorically similar to the sudden force of a nail breaking through a thick partition.

In figure 31, THE MIND IS A CONTAINER metaphor is again evoked. In this example, many ideas stream outward and downward, representing plural lines of thought racing from the mind of a writer in an exuberant display of well-thought-out theories. In this instance, the person writing at the computer had been planning his article for some time, and when he sat down at the desk the brilliant ideas streamed out of his mind effortlessly. The ideas represented in this sign were not half-formed or still being thought over. The metaphorical projection of IDEAS IN EXISTENCE ARE STRAIGHT maps onto the "long, thin objects" emanating from the brain and evokes fully conceived ideas ready to be typed into the computer.

Thoughts are recognized as being abstract. However, even as abstractions, they are thought of as existing or not existing. In ASL, existing thoughts are represented by a straight classifier. Thoughts that are not yet fully conceptualized are seen as being bent or curved. The sign PUZZLE probably lexicalized from the sign QUESTION MARK, which began by tracing an outline of a question mark in the air. Although the bend at the end of the sign formation pragmatically dots the question mark, it also conveys bewilderment.

Figure 31. "Plural-thoughts-stream-from-head"

The meanings of this lexical item do not include "inaccurate." When the hand is placed near the forehead to create the sign PUZ-ZLE, the prominent referent deals with confusion or a lack of understanding. In other words, the person is aware that something is not known or understood. In figure 32, PUZZLE represents understanding that is *not fully in existence.* The sign clearly identifies itself in Quadrant #1 (see chapter 4, table 2) since it is both metaphorical and iconic. Tracing the question mark in the air creates an iconic symbol. The bent finger is also isomorphic with many other objects seen everywhere in nature. Trees, flowers, even animals at times, are hunched over and listless if they are going out of existence or dying. In the opposite stage of development, a flower bud or a newborn is unfurled or curled up, not yet extended fully. The "establishment" or "complete presence" or "existence" of an abstract idea or thought is identified with straightness. The opposite can be iconically represented by something that is bent. IDEAS NOT FULLY IN EX-ISTENCE ARE BENT has many source domain schemas that coherently map onto its abstract target domain and run counter to the IDEAS IN EXISTENCE ARE STRAIGHT metaphor.

Thoughts that are not yet fully conceptualized are seen as being bent or curved. They represent a state of *not being fully in ex-*

Figure 32. PUZZLED

istence. The consultant for figure 33 was asked if the sign for IN-VENT could be articulated with slightly bent fingers. At first his reply was the same as all other consultants who were asked the same question—absolutely not possible. Then he thought it over and decided that it could be done under the guise of a joke. This is a broad translation of his example: "My friends are exceptionally clever people. All of them are inventive and have come up with many novel ideas. I want to invent something, too, but all I seem to be able to do is . . . ." At this point, he signed *INVENT as seen in figure 33.

Whereas INVENT is produced with an upward movement of four rod-straight fingers centered in the middle of the forehead, *INVENT makes the attempt with an upward movement, but seriously flounders when the fingers bend in an unconventional way. The bent fingers conceptually convey the message that whatever invention was desired, the concoction failed miserably. Even though the example was an attempt at humor and was not a conventional way to sign the word, the metaphor IDEAS NOT FULLY IN EXISTENCE ARE BENT was successfully evoked.

Conventional lexical terms also evoke the IDEAS NOT FULLY IN EX-ISTENCE ARE BENT metaphor: PUZZLED*,[13] WEAK-MIND, DREAM, HUH?,

CONFUSE, MULL-OVER, SUSPICIOUS, and others. Each of these signs is articulated with bent fingers.[14] Mapping from one concrete source domain onto the target domain does not preclude mappings of other sorts (Turner 1991, 191). The signs above have composites of metaphorical mappings that vary according to their source domains. Metonyms are also embedded or interpenetrated in each case. Yet the single consistency in all of the signs is the bent finger that alludes to thoughts or ideas that are *not fully existing*. For example, DREAM, with its repetitive straight-to-bent index finger pulling away from the forehead, does not represent clear, coherent thoughts. A source domain of an object slowly drifting away from a central location, as a boat or leaf might pull away from an island, maps onto the target domain of thoughts gliding off into space,

Figure 33. *INVENT

---

13. The asterisk after the gloss indicates that the sign is stressed. This word flexes all four fingers instead of only one, as in the conventional lexical item PUZ-ZLED (see fig. 32).

14. The sign WISE, with its bent index finger tapping downward at the center of the forehead, seems to be motivated by the etymology of a semantically similar sign, SMART. Further information on the phonological and morphological relationships between the two words can be found in Long (1918) and Michaels (1923).

sliding away from the mind. MULL-OVER uses curved, circling fingers and thumbs to indicate thoughts that are still fuzzy and unformed. The source domain of touching each individual object before making a selection, as when shoppers in a store touch pieces of fruit before making a choice on a purchase, maps coherently to the thorough, repetitive contact that the fingers make when considering every thought before making a decision. SUSPICION scratches a bent index finger several times at the "conscious thinking" location on the forehead. Scratching the surface of a mine in search of minerals is not unlike digging at the mind hoping to find more information in order to confirm a hunch. WEAK-MIND has parameters similar to the sign for physically WEAK, except the location is at the forehead. The fingers are lax and fall against the forehead in a bent, weakened manner, mapping the physical domain of a worn-out body to mental stamina. DOUBT is made with the V classifier pulling away from the eyes, yanking downwards and away from the body into two tightly bent fingers. This sign has numerous mappings, one of them being based on KNOWING IS SEEING. The two tightly bent fingers, representing eyes that are no longer able to "see," take on a mapping of blindness. In fact, the sign for BLIND in ASL is articulated with the Bent V classifier. An epistemic form of DOUBT is made with slight repetitive wiggles of the bent fingers, indicating that there is some possibility that the skepticism may not be total.

Tropes interact with each other to create complex structures, as in the cases above. Each sign could be further analyzed in depth to show how the metaphors and metonyms embed and overlap. However, it is important to note that each reflects a common metaphorical source domain: the physical shape of the bent finger. We see these image schemas everywhere in nature. They represent dying or limp objects or brand new creations just unfurling or being born. Image schemas of bent objects that are not fully in existence map on to the target domains of each sign as comprehension that is not fully in existence.

It should be noted that not every sign produced with straight fingers near the brain exemplifies IDEAS IN EXISTENCE ARE STRAIGHT.

For example, consider HEADACHE. The citation form is made by jab-bing two straight index fingers toward each other near the center of the forehead. This variant on HURT is not produced with bent or curved index fingers; they are relatively straight at all times. The meaning clearly has to do with physical sensation. No metaphorical extension takes place; no domains are crossed. The sign simply deals with the subjective physical phenomenon of pain.

A Cross-Linguistic Discussion of UNDERSTAND

One of the broadest goals of the study of linguistics is to determine how human languages are alike and how they are different. Bybee et al. (1994, 1) studied seventy-six spoken languages in order to de-termine their similarities and differences. Signed languages can also benefit from cross-linguistic comparison though different in modal-ity from spoken languages. Some interesting similarities and differ-ences were found in the area of metaphorical mapping during this study.

The English language metaphor **understanding is grasping,** ex-emplified by the expressions "Did you get what he meant?" or "Kassie's got the answer now," was found to be less prevalent in ASL. In ASL, similar instantiations are instead manifested through the rich structural metaphor IDEAS IN EXISTENCE ARE STRAIGHT.[15] If the sign GET (with its grasped handshape) was used instead, what would be implied is a literal, physical act of receiving, rather than an abstract one (i.e., "I GOT THE FAX", but not "I GOT THE IDEA").

However, a cursory glance at several other signed languages indi-cates a diversity of metaphorical mapping where UNDERSTANDING IS GRASPING is concerned. The Catalan Sign Language found in Barcelona inflects the TO-UNDERSTAND sign productively so that any

---

15. The UNDERSTANDING IS SEEING metaphor should not be confused with the fact that seeing has been described by consultants as being a critical element in the ability to perceive, thus understand.

agent can use the "grasp" handshape, thereby exhibiting UNDER-
STANDING IS GRASPING. German Sign Language has several different
variants for the sign TO-UNDERSTAND, and maps UNDERSTANDING
IS GRASPING onto both the northern Germany and Berlin variants. Japanese Sign Language also has several variants for TO-
UNDERSTAND, but—like ASL—most of the common variants do not
make use of the UNDERSTANDING IS GRASPING metaphor. Iranian
Sign Language and Swiss German Sign Language make use of
straight fingers that flash open either toward the center of the forehead or frontward, respectively. These languages do not use a
grasping motion when indicating TO-UNDERSTAND. Cuban Sign Language makes use of the IDEAS IN EXISTENCE ARE STRAIGHT (Straight
G classifier) mapping, but does not use the UNDERSTANDING IS
GRASPING metaphor.

Although the French Sign Language (LSF) sign COMPRENDRE
snaps the index finger, the middle finger, and the thumb shut at the
forehead, in an iconic resemblance of a broad clothespin pinching
shut, the fingers are straight and there is no grasping movement as
exemplified by the shape of a fist. However, LSF does grasp with
the straight fingers and thumbs, thus, the UNDERSTANDING IS GRASP-
ING may be substantiated in LSF through the rigid handshapes, if
not through the grasping fist. The Bangalore variety of Indian Sign
Language also shows a type of grasping, but with straight fingers
only. Bangalore uses no grasping of the fist, although straight handshapes reach outward and pull in toward the forehead. The North
American variants of TO-UNDERSTAND (ASL and LSQ, *langue des
signes quebecoise*) are similar, if not identical. Their initial handshapes begin with what could be considered a grasp, but the final
articulation of the sign indicates that no grasping is realized.

By just looking at a small number of international signed languages, we can determine that the UNDERSTANDING IS GRASPING
metaphor does not appear in all of them, and when it does appear,
the grasping is often modified by the handshape. A cross-linguistic
study is needed to determine how prevalent this metaphorical mapping is in signed languages as opposed to spoken languages.

Further analysis of these metaphors and others will illuminate the extent and etymology of their metaphorical structurings. Identifying the metaphorical representations in ASL, and isolating how they are similar to or different from other signed and spoken languages, may lead to a deeper understanding of the cultural and linguistic differences between languages.

Interaction of Metaphor and Metonymy

Metaphors can coalesce with other metaphors, or with metonyms and similes, to create powerful, dynamic narration. One documented ASL discourse segment of the IDEAS ARE OBJECTS and THE MIND IS A CONTAINER metaphorical theme can be seen in the series of pictures in figure 34. This cluster of mappings shows various ways that an idea can be considered an object, and, as such, is capable of falling, being manipulated, held, and so forth. The series of pictures represents part of a conversation in which the consultant explained that ideas can be placed in the head but may not always remain there. As an example of his folk theory, he offered a hypothetical situation in which an actor is learning his lines for a play.

The initial sign that is being articulated is LINE (fig. 34a), which represents sentences in the script. The extended pinkies serve referential functions and allow one entity to be used for another, thus creating a metonym. The metonymic LINE represents printed words in English that have been written down in a script. Next, the line of words is about to be grasped and removed from the script by the consultant's hand (fig. 34b). While the metonymic nature is still in play in the form of printed words being conceptually suspended horizontally in the space in front of the speaker, metaphorical conceptualization occurs also because the hypothetical words (thoughts) are physically unable to remain suspended in the air while waiting to be moved. Thoughts cannot be moved literally. The source domain of physical manipulation is transferred to the target domain of abstract ideas (i.e., the invisible printed words), creating a metaphorical extension.

141

METAPHORICAL MAPPING IN ASL

(a)   (b)   (c)

(d)   (e)

(f)   (g)   (h)

Figure 34. IDEAS ARE OBJECTS

The next picture (fig. 34c) shows "words" from the previous metaphorical, metonymic LINE being held by the Flat O verb stem ("handle a thin flattish wide object") and moved toward the forehead. Selection of this specific handle classifier represents plurality of the words of the sentence that were "taken from" the script. Picking out only one word or one single idea might have necessitated the selection of a different verb handle, possibly the F classifier ("careful discriminating selection from among a host of possible alternates"). The functional reference is to manipulation and control of the objects being moved.

The fourth picture (fig. 34d) shows the consultant signing the imperative STAY. The inward palm orientation indicates an effort to command the scripted words to remain in his head, a metaphorical container for the mind. Personification is evoked here in order to allow the comprehension of abstract containment in human terms. Each instance of personification allows for the selection of different human aspects—motivations, characteristics, or activities—to map onto a nonhuman object. Actually, this metaphor encourages us to conceptualize an animal, possibly a puppy, being ordered to "stay" in one place until released by command. We conceive of the source referent used in dog obedience-training classes to map onto the target concept of an idea being ordered to remain permanently bound at one location in the mind.

The next picture (fig. 34e) shows that the consultant has shifted discourse position to his left in order to indicate that an unexpected conversation is taking place with an imaginary person at his side. Suddenly, the ideas that were ordered to remain within his head are knocked out. The consultant "lost" control of the words that he had metaphorically placed in his head, and the previously bounded words were knocked out due to the topic change during discourse with the imaginary agent.

An idea or a thought, as predicted by the "long, thin object" handshape, can be seen projecting from the consultant's forehead (fig. 34f). All of the mappings previously attributed to the G classifier handshape (see fig. 28)—straightness, IDEAS ARE OBJECTS, IDEAS IN EXISTENCE ARE STRAIGHT, and IDEAS ARE SUBJECT TO FORCE—are manifested in this icon, which is also a metaphor for physical life. Because the handshape represents thoughts that had been metaphorically placed into the mind during memorization of the script, the icon is also a metonym for the "scripted" words from the earlier metaphor.

The sign FALL-FROM-HEAD (figs. 34g and 34h) is articulated in part by the V classifier handshape in order to carry out and complete the action of the line from the script as it metaphorically falls from the consultant's head. The falling thought or idea does not in any sense possess "two legs." TO-FALL can be used to represent a sudden downward motion responding to gravitational pull for any kind of animate or inanimate object, literal or metaphorical, whether it is an elephant, a fork, or an idea. The frozen sign is a generic sign for showing the gravitational pull upon an object (see fig. 35). Although this sign can literally express a person with two legs falling from a flat plane, the metaphorical sign has lost its literal sense of two lower appendages. TO-FALL is one of many commonly used signs standardized in form across signers, "with internal morphological analysis no longer applied" (Supalla 1978, 41). This is in keeping with McDonald's proposal that frozen forms represent

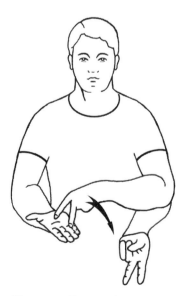

Figure 35. Frozen sign: TO-FALL

greater semantic opacity and wider distributional occurrence (Mc-Donald 1982, 145).

The interaction of the cluster of metaphors and metonyms shown in figure 34 shows the rich discourse that can come from ASL. The spatial mappings that are highlighted in the various expressions—the movement of thoughts, the selection and placement of ideas from one location to another, a fixed and bounded mental animal, discourse shifting, an idea falling from a container into open space—demonstrate the creative dynamics of ASL. In his discussion of how people structure space and motion, Fauconnier says that the "manipulation of space configurations in the absence of a real-world matchup . . . is a major factor behind some unusual aspects of human creativity" (1997, 69). This everyday description of ASL discourse dealing with the thought and language domain demonstrates remarkable language instantiations and creates powerful discourse structures.

Another example of rich tropic interaction was found in the FILE-CABINET simile pictured in figure 8 (see chapter 4). The consultant used the sign OPEN-DRAWER to serve as a container that was mentally structured within the mind. Both metaphorical and metonymic mappings occur with the file cabinet example. The file cabinet icon became a metonymic extension of the brain—a storehouse for thoughts that interpreters must rifle through in order to select the right concept. Thoughts cannot literally be placed into a drawer and stored for later use. However, the source domain of physically lifting folders from a sliding drawer maps onto the target domain of thoughts being lifted out of an abstract thought process.

This juxtaposition of the literal and the abstract domains creates an interesting metaphor. The metonymic mapping occurring simultaneously in OPEN-DRAWER is revealed by the A_s (fist) handshape that is used to represent the handle of the drawer, a metonym for the entire drawer itself. The Open C classifier is a metonym for the side of the drawer, which also metonymically represents the whole drawer, and subsequently, the entire file cabinet. The OPEN-DRAWER represents a creative subordinate metaphor for THE MIND IS A CONTAINER.

Metaphorical entailments interact with other tropic components in powerful and creative ways. These interactions provide structural continuity that supply conventional as well as novel messages that work in fluid cognitive processes. Instead of being separate, isolated figures of speech, the tropes are unbounded linguistic participants of conceptual construction. The mental spaces of a metaphor generate multiple readings and multiple tropic projections (Fauconnier 1997, 54). ASL tropic components create fluid interpretations that are as rich and as novel as those in any spoken language.

6

CROSSING A
METAPHORICAL OCEAN

What mysteries are embedded in a sign? The simplest signs in ASL have passed through the hands of thousands of deaf people. The motions have been repeated millions of times. What happens to the shape and to the meaning of common signs in ASL when they have been expressed and embodied daily by deaf people? What metaphors have mapped onto the knuckles, fingers, skin, and bones of a sign?

In chapter 5 the Flat O classifier handshape was shown to manipulate and move thoughts and ideas metaphorically, as in the metaphor IDEAS ARE OBJECTS TO BE MANIPULATED OR PLACED. This handle verb has also acquired a prototypical "frozen" sense and can mean to pass an object from one person or place to another, in other words, TO-GIVE. The common, frequently used sign in ASL has a semantic frame that is rich and linguistically vigorous. The diachronic mappings of the sign GIVE evolved from a simple classifier in early French sign language to a discourse marker in ASL that currently has no literal connotation, only metaphorical mapping. Examining how one ASL sign slowly crossed literal and metaphorical oceans can provide us with a deeper understanding of how all signs in ASL evolve and become richer semantic forms.

The most basic act of giving is the transfer of control of an object from one person to another. The act of giving is frequent, requires purposeful human interaction, and is central to human experience. In spoken languages, *giving* has morphemes that show the parts that compose the act of giving: the giver, the thing, the recipient (Newman 1998). Corresponding morphemes are also found in the variants of the ASL sign GIVE.

146

The *giving* frame (the semantic envelope that includes the giver, the thing, and the recipient) in ASL is both literal and metaphorical. The two main forms of the ASL *giving* frame and their respective variants, GIVE₁ and GIVE₂, can convey both literal and abstract concepts. An investigation of the GIVE₂ morpheme revealed semantic connections between the acts of giving in ASL and in *langue des signes françaises* (French Sign Language, or LSF). The verb stem phonology of both morphemes has a common etymology but diverge functionally. A purely metaphorical variant—GIVE₂-*concede*— serves as a discourse marker that is used to change the course of an ASL conversation. It no longer means to give an object to another person.

The data for this chapter came from both native and near-native users of ASL. Native users of ASL comprise less than 8 percent of the total deaf population. Only a small percentage of deaf children are born of deaf parents who sign ASL. Thus, in the interest of descriptive linguistics and to examine how GIVE is used in the general Deaf community, this author included a number of language consultants who learned the language in the manner of over 90 percent of the deaf population—through later acquisition, rather than from birth. The one hearing consultant was the sole hearing member in an all-Deaf family. There is debate over what constitutes American Sign Language. Because I was interested in how the *giving* frame is used sociolinguistically by members of the Deaf community, signs that occurred naturally in the data were accepted as being representative of normal ASL discourse. All consultants for the GIVE study have been using the language daily for over twenty years and are considered to be fluent and intuitive users of ASL.

Prototype GIVE₁

In ASL, the physical hand itself (not an iconic reference) and its patterned configurations and path movements are crucial to the semantic construction of the prototypical verb GIVE₁ (see fig. 36).[1]

---

1. Graphics in chapter 6 were produced by Sherman Wilcox.

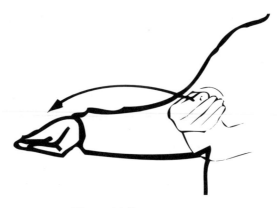

Figure 36. Prototype GIVE₁

The phonological form of the handshape that represents an object can provide size and shape information about the thing being transmitted. The path movement indicates the relationship between the arguments and their agreement for location. Verb signs move back and forth between the referents when marking co-reference (van Hoek 1992). The prototype's path of motion typically follows a slight arc flowing upward from the giver then downward toward the recipient. There are other variants of the arc and path of motion of GIVE₁ (such as the arc that begins with the palm down, smoothly flowing into a palm flipped upward and outward toward the recipient), but they are not described in this chapter.

In figure 36, the classifier verb stem "handle a thin flattish wide object" is realized in the prototypical verb GIVE₁. Other classifier handshapes can also be designated when handling an object being given to someone, but this particular handle configuration has acquired a frozen status in ASL for the passing of any literal object from one person to another.

One study on ASL spatial language use—how people talk about space—suggests that the primary function of handle verbs of motion is to express a change in location and direction for an inanimate object, rather than expressing the way an object should be held (Emmorey and Casey 1995). In other words, when ASL users were asked to solve a set of spatial puzzles, the handle classifiers were not used as instructions for how to hold an object (in this case, a block) but for *movement* instructions instead. This emphasis on movement suggests that the shape of the hands may be used to identify the shape of an object being specified, but a more salient linguistic function can override the iconicity of the handshape form.

This linguistic override operates in metaphorical extension in the *giving* frame. For example, GIVE$_1$ provides information about (1) control over the object, (2) the change of location from a giver to a recipient, and (3) the size and shape of an object. A message can indicate that a flat, thin thing—such as a piece of paper—is being passed between people. However, when GIVE$_1$ operates under the status of a frozen sign, further linguistic function is found—the movement of an abstraction becomes more salient than size and shape. As the sign has become more frozen and more acceptable as a vehicle for literally moving any *thing* between people, mentally conceived objects, as well as literal objects, have become passable. Extended metaphorical abstractions such as a language or the values of a culture can be passed on by using what was originally a handle classifier for a thin, flattish, wide object. This semantic change follows the conventional generalization that such change proceeds from the concrete to the abstract (Traugott 1974, 1982; Traugott and Konig 1991; Sweetser 1990).

Typically, the handle handshape realized in GIVE$_1$ can represent the giving of common objects ranging from the size of small keys to kitchen chairs. Other classifier (CL) handshapes, called size or shape specifiers (Baker and Cokely 1980), can represent nouns such as GLASS or CUP. Janzen (1995) notes that classifiers often select a property of the noun (such as shape) to describe, and so may act in a sense like adjectives. When giving someone a glass of water, for example, the CL:*cylindrical* (a classifier that takes on a similar shape and size of the container) can be selected.

Thus, specific hand configurations for giving an object, such as a videocassette or a candlestick, can be encoded. The hand forms an isomorphic shape of an object enclosed by the palm, fingers, and thumb and presents an iconic image of the conceived thing that is being mentally "held." Not every conceivable handshape is acceptable; there are patterned and conventionalized shapes. The signer

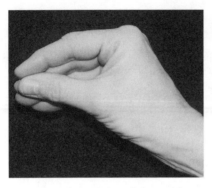 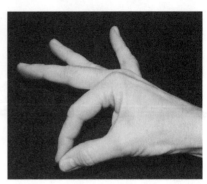

"thin, flattish, wide handle" morpheme   F morpheme

Figure 37. Handshape variations used in the *giving* frame

decides during discourse which classificatory features will be used. However, for the everyday occurrence of passing an object from a giver to a recipient, the frozen Flat O morpheme depicted in figure 37 is generally selected.

As previously described in Newman 1998, this prototypical *giving* frame in ASL differs from another polysynthetic language, Chipewyan. The spoken Athapaskan language obligatorily encodes shape verb stems with a near absence of either neutral or generic statements of *giving* (Rice 1998). ASL does frequently encode and emphasize shapes of objects being passed, but it also maintains a prototype for the *giving* frame in general. Chipewyan rarely makes use of figurative extension when giving; ASL accepts metaphorical mapping in its *giving* frame.

Change of Control

In GIVE$_1$ predicates a strong sense of possession is not obligatory. A change of control over an object is the salient semantic sense commonly understood in the prototypical *giving* act in ASL. This distinction can be illustrated in an example from my data (Wilcox 1998, 181). A consultant made use of the Flat O handshape (see fig. 37) to explain that her mother had passed a needle to a friend during a monthly craft and sewing session. The consultant could have used an alternative classifier verb stem that means "handle a small or flattish object" (such as a seed or a piece of lint). If this had been the case, the F morpheme (see fig. 37) would have been used (McDonald 1982). But the salient meaning in this situation had to do with the passing of the needle from one person to another. The size or shape of the object was not a critical aspect of the message. Therefore, the Flat O morpheme of the prototype verb $GIVE_1$ was selected, rather than a classifier that would have shown a more explicit shape and size of the needle being passed.

When a classifier is used primarily for descriptive purposes, the handshapes selected can give an indication of the size or the shape of that object. But in the $GIVE_1$ prototype construct, because the handshape has acquired a frozen status, the function becomes highlighted. There is still a weak isomorphic mapping of size and shape to be found in the handshape form, but the primary intent of $GIVE_1$ is the function of passing a thing from a giver to a recipient, resulting in a change of control.

Change of Location

Typically, in ASL, people who are conceived as being physically present are associated with loci corresponding to their spatial locations in front of the signer. Langacker refers to this particular mental space representation as the *current discourse space* (1991, 97). Mental spaces are conceptual representations that are set up as people talk or listen to one another and are used to structure various roles, strategies, and relations (Fauconnier 1985, 1). In ASL, the person to be discussed is referenced by the use of indexing (pointing in the direction of the conceptualized person or object with the index finger).

A signer who sets up a prototypical $GIVE_1$ construct indicates that an object will be handed over (by articulating the sign and the appropriate nonmanual markers for that object) in a distributional process that occurs sequentially from a starting point agent to an endpoint agent. Thus, the conceived object that is passed from giver to recipient is passed physically, as well as temporally, from one mental space to another. Typically, a giver begins the sign by moving her hand from the center of her own signing space toward the center of the recipient's signing space. A signer can give a conceived thing, such as a calendar or a CD-ROM, to a person directly in front of her by extending the GIVE$_1$ verb stem toward that person, just as though an actual item were being offered. Commonly accepted ASL discourse practice for using a nonpresent referent has a subject and an object mentally "set-up" in space before the verb is realized, allowing the verb to take an object. Thus, the hand is extended outward toward the nonpresent recipient to indicate giving to some mentally conceived referent.

An uninflected GIVE$_1$ prototype that shows the basic passing of an object from first-person singular to second-person singular can be further inflected to indicate a *giving* scene of multiple indeterminate agents and objects (Klima and Bellugi 1979, 300–15). Physical objects such as books, videocassettes, or objects the size of a chair are readily passed from giver to recipient by the use of the prototype morpheme. Relatively small objects of no great monetary or sentimental value are also passed from giver to recipient. The consultants for this study felt there was a restriction on size with the use of this morpheme, however. For example, its acceptance was ambiguous when used to give an automobile. The morpheme could be used, but is rarer. Typically, the GIVE$_1$ morpheme was not used to refer to giving a car to someone (see Wilcox 1998 for further analysis of this morpheme).

Another object that did not readily accept the GIVE$_1$ morpheme was the giving of a house. Folk explanations behind this restriction indicated that a house was "too large" or "too valuable" to be used in connection with that morpheme. This constriction complies with the earlier functional sense applied to the prototype morpheme—it is used to *pass* an object from one person to another. Only when a house is given from one family member to another in a type of transmission by *inheritance* is the GIVE$_1$ morpheme typically acceptable. Consultants indicated that a different morpheme would be more appropriate for giving something the size and the value of a home (see discussion of GIVE$_2$).

GIVE$_1$-*completive*

Often acting in concurrence with GIVE$_1$ in many discourse situations is a completive verb that is similar to the prototype. The only phonological difference appears to be a final motion bound to the main verb stem morpheme. The sign ends with an opening extension of the fingers and thumb in an act of "flinging out contents." Analysis indicates that it often has to do with either plurality or the sense of finality. "Perhaps plurality is associated with the completive sense because to carry an activity or process through to completion, in many cases, would involve affecting multiple patients" (Bybee et al. 1994, 60). The GIVE$_1$-*completive* morpheme is often associated with the distribution of things to an unspecified number of recipients. The sign can be articulated with two hands bent inward toward the waist, moving from the center signing space outwardly in arcs. The GIVE$_1$-*completive* begins its articulation with the handle classifier and ends with the completive morpheme. This sign accepts literal objects.

However, making a location change to the forehead, the GIVE$_1$-*completive* can pass on abstract ideas, information, and opinions. No literal objects are given when the sign is moved near the brain. As such, the GIVE sign is commonly glossed as TO-INFORM or INFORMATION and assumes a totally metaphorical nature.

The end morpheme of GIVE$_1$-*completive* strongly resembles the phonological morpheme found at the end of the ASL sign FINISH. Although not identical, the form–meaning similarity between the two is striking. The sense of thoroughly and completely releasing or passing an object to someone is found in GIVE$_1$-*completive*. Literal objects of various sizes can be given with GIVE$_1$-*completive*. Further research is needed to determine the strength of metaphorical extension on this morpheme and what abstractions can be conveyed with its use. If an object is expected to become a valued permanent possession of the recipient, GIVE$_1$-*completive* is often accompanied by another GIVE construction that adds this additional information to the discourse (see discussion of GIVE$_2$ below).

Give$_2$

As demonstrated previously, GIVE$_1$ serves as a prototype for the *giving* frame in general. Although money can be passed by the use of the GIVE$_1$ morpheme, more typically, a different morpheme is used (see fig. 38). GIVE$_2$ is similar to the prototype verb in some aspects but contributes additional semantic information due to the phonemic verb stem difference.

Permanent Possession, Money, and Value

The path of motion between the conventional arguments of GIVE$_2$ retains the semantic senses of *passing* and of *change of control*, which are congruent with the prototypical GIVE frame. However, whereas the GIVE$_1$ morpheme does not assume a strong sense of possession, GIVE$_2$ does. This distinction is also found in the spoken language Sochiapan Chinantec, when one construction refers to a temporary transfer of an object, and a second construction is used when the act of giving is irrevocable and the thing truly becomes the possession of the recipient (Newman 1996, 267).

GIVE$_2$ involves several semantic extensions and motivates the senses of *permanent possession, money,* and *value*. The GIVE$_2$ morpheme is often used when something is given to a recipient with the expectation that the person will retain control over the object

Figure 38. GIVE$_2$

and not pass it on to someone else. In contrast, everyday giving in which an object is passed on to another person without the expectation that it will remain permanently with that recipient makes use of GIVE$_1$. There is a general distinction between the two handshape morphemes. Their meanings are often fluid and used interchangeably, yet several semantic distinctions can be found.

If a person chooses the GIVE$_2$ morpheme when giving an object—say a jacket—to a recipient, the person receiving the jacket would assume that the article of clothing should not be passed on to another person. The handshape morpheme implies a permanent ownership role and the recipient understands they are being given a "gift" rather than just an object. Permanent possession becomes salient with this verb stem. The recipient has more than a temporary change of control over the jacket. It becomes his *to own and to keep* if he wants. This sense of permanent possession is not motivated directly by the handshape of the GIVE$_2$ verb stem morpheme. Its etymology is more complex than an isomorphic classifier representation, although there are vestiges of iconicity in its distant past.

Direct, causal links in the historical evolution of lexical items in ASL have been difficult to document. The few writing systems mentioned earlier in this book (Newkirk 1987; Stokoe, Casterline, and Croneberg 1976; Sutton 1981) are not commonly used by native signers in the Deaf community. However, there is a documented historical relationship between ASL and LSF (Lane 1984). This typological relationship is found between the ASL verb, GIVE$_2$, and in several signs relating to money in LSF.

A number of lexical items in LSF that relate to money appear to have evolved from the physical shape for coins found in the earlier money signs preserved in Lambert (1865). At that time there were a large number of LSF signs with unmarked handshapes; only a few were articulated with tight, complex, marked handshapes. Of those few, three were related to money: *argent, sous,* and *franc.* The modern LSF sign for "money" looks like a mimed gesture of rubbing the thumb with the fingers to show coins or paper notes in a palm. Many modern LSF signs that deal with money make use of a tight

X-form handshape, which is phonologically similar to the earlier nineteenth-century signs. Three such money-related signs are found in figure 39 (Moody 1986a, 1986b; Girod 1997a, 1997b): ACHETER (buy), CHER (expensive), and DONNER UNE SUBVENTION (subsidy). Some other phonologically related signs (not pictured) are L'ARGENT (money), BANQUE (bank), DÉPENSER (to spend), DONNER-UN-DESSOUS-DE-TABLE (to bribe), FAIRE DES COURSES (to go shopping), FAIRE-UN-COLLECTION (to collect), MOINS CHER (less expensive), REM-BOURSER (to reimburse), and PRÊTER (to lend).

The phonological and semantic evolutions of the GIVE$_2$ verb demonstrate an extension from the LSF signs that denote money.[2] The tight X-form phoneme in the LSF signs that deal with money is similar to the looser, extended X-form of the GIVE$_2$ morpheme. However, there is little physical resemblance between the verb stem morphemes of GIVE$_2$ and the LSF sign for *give*, DONNER. DONNER, with a Flat O morpheme, is phonologically identical to the ASL prototype GIVE$_1$. Nevertheless, the verb stem that ASL users often select for the giving of money or financial donations is the loose X-form morpheme, rather than the Flat O verb stem.

Words do not randomly acquire new meanings. Sweetser explains, "The multiple synchronic senses of a given word will

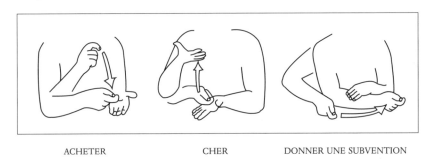

ACHETER   CHER   DONNER UNE SUBVENTION

Figure 39. LSF money-related signs

2. I am grateful for the contributions of the actors at the International Visual Theatre, Centre Socio Cultural Des Sourdes, Vincennes, France: Carole Guttian, Chantal Liennel, Simon Attia, Jerome Caillon, and Jean-Yves Augros.

normally be related to each other in a motivated fashion" (1990, 9). The composite senses of GIVE$_2$ indicate that the path of motion between arguments supports the sense of *passing* and *change of control* found in the prototype. Additionally, the X-form handshape does not have an explicit size or shape classifier sense attached to it. Objects of *any* size or shape are typically given through the use of this verb stem. However, all consultants in this study indicated that GIVE$_2$ was often associated with the passing, the giving, or the donation of money. Not one consultant expressed the opinion that the handshape may have come from any of the specific LSF signs listed above. But each insisted that the sign was money-related. Several consultants offered the opinion that the money sense found in the X-form handshape may have arisen "long ago."[3]

The folk etymology of the consultants mirrors what we can surmise about the physical form of the GIVE$_2$ verb stem; it is visually similar to a large number of signs having to do with money in LSF. A semantic extension for money has mapped onto the prototype ASL sign for GIVE$_1$ via the X-form from LSF and motivates a semantic distinction between the two main ASL TO-GIVE signs.

Taking the diachronic study of GIVE$_2$ further reveals an interesting LSF sign that demonstrates the diverse path that semantics may take. The LSF sign RENDRE HOMAGE (to pay one's respect to someone) is metaphorically derived from the gesture for tipping one's hat ("tire son chapeau à" in spoken French). RENDRE HOMAGE uses the tight X-form handshape, representing a classifier shape for grasping the brim of a hat. Girod (1997b) indicates that the long movement demonstrates "an idea of the intensity of the respect." Metaphorically, it also indicates that the sense of respect is being permanently offered, with no withdrawal forthcoming. It may be impossible to

---

3. ASL is historically related to LSF. In the early nineteenth century, Laurent Clerc, a young deaf teacher from Paris, France, was persuaded by Thomas Hopkins Gallaudet, a Protestant minister, to travel to the United States and establish the first permanent American school for deaf children in Hartford, Connecticut. The language taught by Clerc mixed with the indigenous signed languages used by his young American students to become modern ASL (Lane 1984).

determine exactly where the sense of permanent possession that is found in GIVE₂ comes from. Yet the semantic paths found in the phonologically and morphologically similar LSF sign RENDRE HOMAGE seem to flow metaphorically into this ASL *giving* verb.

Metonymy is also realized in the verb stems representing the French words for money. The tight-X symbolizes the part of the hand holding the coin or bill. In many examples, objects are metonymically conceived by virtue of the handshape handling an object. Yet metonymy can also operate on the more abstract level in the *giving* frame. The leading principle of metonymy is contiguity, in which something is in the state of being continuous. Metonymic change is also correlated with shifts in meaning situated in the subjective belief state or when expressing a speaker's attitude toward a situation (Hopper and Traugott 1993, 87). An excellent example of this variety of metonymic change in the *giving* frame occurs in a regional offshoot of the ASL sign GIVE₂. In North Carolina, deaf signers use the GIVE₂ systematically and conventionally, as other ASL native signers in the United States do. However, a sign that recently emerged in the North Carolina lexicon corresponds with the English word "crook." This newly coined sign retains the form of GIVE₂, with its predicate verb stem, loose-X. However, the motion in this sign changes drastically. Whereas conventional TO-GIVE verbs identify arguments through a change of location, this sign does not travel from a giver toward a recipient. There is no change of control via the movement. Instead, the motion resembles the rap of a hammer, and the sign is articulated low at the waist, slightly below the conventionalized signing space. Metaphors that we generate for morality are motivated by our physical experiences. The orientational mapping in this sign represents the Moral Strength Metaphor that equates being low with being bad (Lakoff and Johnson 1999, 300). Grounding this CROOK sign with a metaphorically low movement still retains the sense of money through the handshape. However, the passing motion is eliminated from the lexical item. The motion morpheme is where the semantic change take place. The passing motion becomes substituted with the downward rap that signifies a detrimental act. Because this sign is used to refer to a person, the standard GIVE$_2$ verb has evolved into a noun representing a noxious person that people must be wary of.

A third sense pervading the everyday use of GIVE$_2$ is that of perceived *value*. An object can be given with this verb stem even when there is no monetary worth involved—if the item is valued by the giver or the receiver. A grandfather might use the GIVE$_2$ sign when giving his grandson a handcarved wooden car, knowing that the boy will enjoy playing with the toy. Another example of this sense of value within the GIVE$_2$ sign took place at a monthly crafts meeting. A deaf woman was making a small craft and noticed that her seamstress friend had some tiny strands of Spanish moss that would make a lovely attachment to her own handiwork. She asked her friend if she could borrow a piece of moss until able to buy some of her own. The second deaf woman insisted that under no circumstances would it be necessary to repay her; she would GIVE$_2$ the moss to her friend. Moss is of little monetary worth. Yet, because one woman needed the moss, the other person realized its value and gave the moss to her friend on the basis of valued abstraction. This sense seems to derive subtly from the meaning of money and its importance and value in society; the form of the handshape retains the *sense* of the value of money even though no money is involved.

GIVE$_2$-*formal* (Nonrotated Wrist)

Metaphorical extension can operate on a sign though the movement of the wrist. Rotation of the wrist occurs when the GIVE$_2$ verb stem is used to give common items such as an inexpensive hair dryer or a comic book. Our understanding of the abstract, mental world is modeled through our pragmatic experience with the physical world. The flexible rotation of the wrist corresponds with the everyday experience of flexibility and limp execution that we observe in our own interactions when routinely passing objects to one another.

However, there are times when the *giving* wrist loses this lax rotation and instead displays firm stiffness. The speed operating along the path of motion of the arms also becomes generally slower. Additionally, both hands are sometimes used—thus motivating a sense of formality in the *giving* frame. This slower, deliberately tense presentation of an object motivates the GIVE₂-*formal* verb.

GIVE₂-*formal* is usually reserved for special occasions or for the awarding of a gift that honors a person or group. The stiffness of the wrist iconically relates to the sense of formality found in the bestowing of an award. People usually put on special clothing or don more artifacts when conducting ceremonies of any kind. The occasional redundant use of two hands supports a notion of ceremony. One constant found in extremely formal *giving* presentations is the high extended arcing of the path of motion. The extra hand, the high arc movement, and the additional time expended into the articulation of the GIVE₂-*formal* is different from everyday *giving* functions.

When the GIVE₂-*formal* morpheme is used to represent money, it can designate the giving of large financial sums such as grants from a government agency, large donations to a nonprofit corporation, or an award of a substantial amount. Giving a friend a five-dollar bill can be articulated with GIVE₂ (lax wrist); being awarded a National Science Foundation grant rates the use of the GIVE₂-*formal* variant.

Metaphorical Extension, Time Line, and De-iconization

Many semantic extensions for *give* are found in English. Newman (1994, 13) points out the following examples:

1. give (advice, opinion, etc.) = "to express (advice, opinion, etc.) to someone"
2. give one's word = "to promise"
3. give permission, consent, etc. = "to permit"
4. give a hand = "to help"
5. give a push = "to push"
6. give a punch = "to punch"

When looking at the prevalence of metaphorical extension in GIVE signs in ASL, "equivalents" of the above English phrases (with the exception of the first one) do not include either of the verb stem morphemes of GIVE₁ or GIVE₂ as described in this chapter. However, there are ways to express, for example, the "giving of a promise" in ASL. This is what is referred to as an "equivalent" above. Research is needed to determine how cognitively extended the GIVE variants are. However, most ASL equivalents of these English expressions are produced with an outward motion from the first person. Newman (1996) discusses the literal emergence of an object coming from a zone of some sort. He describes an abstract motion of a thing out of a sphere of control, or imaginary boundary, around the giver. In some languages the meaning of *give* expressions has been built upon this kind of emergence of some entity from another. This abstract motion motivates the metaphorical extensions of the English giving frame.

In ASL the past is generally conceived as being located slightly behind the signer's body, with the future being represented in the space in front of the body. Most descriptions of the general passing of genetic heritages are described with the prototype verb stem arcing along a type of metaphorical *time line*. The distant past as a source of the hereditary trait maps on to the temporal sense of the time line. In discussing inheritance the GIVE$_1$ morpheme is commonly initiated at the shoulder of the signer, with either one or two hands arcing downward. Each arc endpoint represents a mentally conceived domain of a generation, or a person from that generation. Thus, the GIVE$_1$ construct of heritage shows agreement with present or nonpresent arguments, and metaphorically maps onto the abstraction of time.

In *langue des signes française,* hereditary gifts map onto the same time line. The handshape used is different, however. Physical objects that are passed on by the deceased to family or friends, such as money or a home, will map on to the same time line found in ASL, but the handshape does not resemble any of the ASL GIVE forms. Instead, the handshapes for the French hereditary sign look like two fists in tight contact, one on top of the other, as though both are holding tightly to an upright stick. This is how money or houses are passed on via inheritance. This two-hand sign arches downward from the shoulder as though smoothly passing a physical object from one point on the time line to the next. If a very small but precious item such as a ring, or a genetic trait such as deafness or eye-color is being passed on, or even the passing on of signed language, the same time line is followed; but the hand-shapes change to what looks like the G classifier found in ASL, the "thin, long object" fingers.

Boyes-Braem refers to an ongoing "de-iconization" process in signed language in which the handshape parameter increasingly prefers variants not marked by the grasp element feature (1981, 22). Thus, if the grasp is deleted, the sign becomes "de-pantomimed." Frishberg (1976) provides historical evidence for this de-pantomization of the handshape through the dropping of a +Grasp feature. The Old French Sign Language sign for "thing" used a Grasping O handshape, whereas the modern ASL sign uses a Flat B (5) hand-shape. Frishberg also provides evidence that ASL moves steadily from the concrete to the more abstract. In modern LSF the mor-pheme carrying some objects along the heritage time line still makes use of the fist, or +Grasp, feature. However, ASL prefers the morpheme found in GIVE$_1$. Research into the grammaticalization of the metaphorical time lines of both languages, ASL and LSF, needs to be done to determine whether "de-pantomization" of the re-spective morphemes is occurring.

Metaphorical Interaction between GIVE$_1$ and GIVE$_2$-formal

The next example shows TO-GIVE signs being used interchangeably in metaphorical senses, with no literal transferal taking place. A deaf activist was performing before an audience of mostly young deaf adults. At the end of his performance, he confided to the audi-ence that his mother—whom many people in the theater knew—had recently passed away. He spoke lovingly about the deaf pride that she had instilled in him as a young boy. He explained that it had been his mother who had given him the sign language that he now used to entertain others, the knowledge of Deaf culture that he cherished, the sense of humor that he used to overcome life's ob-stacles, and his understanding of deaf heritage and history. After telling the audience all of this, he signed:

MOTHER $_{\text{right [two hands]}}$GIVE$_{\text{1center}}$ L-E-G-A-C-Y $_{\text{right [two hands]}}$GIVE$_2$-*formally*$_{\text{center}}$

[role shift] $_{\text{center[two hands]}}$GIVE$_{\text{1(audience)}}$ center[two hands]$^{}$GIVE$_2$-*formally*$_{\text{(audience)}}$.

"Mother gave me a true gift, a legacy, and I, in turn, have passed it on to other deaf people."

In this example, cultural abstractions are being given—language, heritage, history. The abstract directionality is explicit. The mental image of the mother was situated higher than the actor himself, reflecting either his remembrance of his mother being taller when he was a child receiving these "gifts," or his sense of his mother being now in heaven. The abstract cultural elements that his mother gave him moved downward into his signing space, then passed on in a canonical encounter to the audience in front of him.

Meaning is not reduced to objective characterization alone; the person chooses how to construe the situation and express it to others (Langacker 1991, 315). In the metaphorical scene above, the actor's mother did not physically give him anything that he could literally pass on to the audience. Metaphors are conceptual mappings. The source domain concept of a physical object mapped onto the abstract target domain concept of the historical "thing"—heritage, culture, language. These abstractions were then metaphorically passed on in much the same way that one would give food or clothing to others. This semantic extension enables abstract ideas about culture or language to be given from one person to another in ASL.

Metaphorical GIVE$_2$-*concede*

Physical objects are rarely involved when the GIVE$_2$-*concede* construction is executed (see fig. 40). Nothing is literally given to another person. The context surrounding this sign usually involves a small squabble, a dispute, or an argument over an obscure point. The disagreement might be over an abstraction such as who is the more talented movie actress, or what is the color of a new car, or which is the correct spelling of a word. It is possible for a physical object to be involved in the discourse surrounding this verb, but the physical object itself is of secondary importance. If the argument evolves around who gets to keep some item, even though someone

Figure 40. GIVE₂-*concede*

eventually gives in and allows another person to have the item in question, the argument and subsequent deferral itself is the primary focus when GIVE₂-*concede* is used. The person who decides to stop arguing over an object willingly allows the other interlocutor to assume possession of the thing. But the type of argument in which an object is actually the focus of the debate is rare.

More typically, an abstract, argumentative point is ceded. For example, two people sitting in an office might both see a young clerk walk past the door. One person comments on her orange hair color, while the other insists that it was light pink. This difference of opinion might continue for a minute or two until one person, out of exasperation, uses the GIVE₂-*concede* sign, implying, "Ok, ok, have it your way—it's pink!"

The handshape is identical for both GIVE₂ and GIVE₂-*concede*. Yet the two signs differ in important ways. In GIVE₂, there is usually a slight rotation of the wrist as the verb stem leaves the center of the giver's space domain and is directed toward the mental space domain of the recipient. In a GIVE₂-*concede* construct, there is typically no rotation of the wrist.[4] The wrist movement is stiffened and the

---

4. The author has seen a variant articulated with a smaller movement and with wrist rotation; the semantics of this form needs to be examined. However, all the examples offered by the consultants in this study were of the type noted above; therefore, discussion will center on that variant.

movement arc is long and extended (more similar to GIVE$_2$-*formal* than to GIVE$_2$ with its rotated wrist). The most interesting aspect is the initial location. In a metaphorical representation of the distancing that the giver feels when deciding to cede an argument, the GIVE$_2$-*concede* verb stem originates away from the giver's own body. The meaning of this sign is clear: I am giving up something to you, but it is not from the "heart." Neither is it from the central signing space. The sign construct usually begins over the shoulder of the dominant hand. It ends in the same location as the other TO-GIVE verbs—the endpoint of the arc travels toward the recipient.

Additional nonmanual markers support the iconicity of this metaphorical giving act. If an argument becomes slightly heated before the giver decides to cede a point, the giver may not look into the eyes of the recipient—one of the few times that eye contact does not take place between the participants in ASL *giving* frames. In addition, the chin may tilt either upward or downward, but definitely back and off to the side, physically and metaphorically distancing the giver from the recipient.

The sign WILLING often precedes GIVE$_2$-*concede*. But the message conveyed is a grudging form of giving. Even though an argumentative point is given "willingly" on the part of the giver, it is not given "wholeheartedly." The message strongly suggests that it is given for the sake of expediency or peacekeeping rather than generosity.

GIVE$_2$-*concede* has acquired the grammatical role of a discourse marker. An example of this act of transition occurred in the data when two friends were having an argument that continued at length because one person wanted very much to get her point across. Eventually, her friend decided to stop the discussion, signing that he would "GIVE$_2$-*concede*" the argument to her. She quickly inflected that verb, executing it as though it had come from his direction toward herself, then shook her head to protest that she adamantly refused to accept an end to the argument. She insisted on continuing the discussion until she could make her point understood. In this example, GIVE$_2$-*concede* was used not only to "give in" a metaphorical point to a friend, but as an indication that the discussion was about to end. The woman was not fooled by the GIVE₂ handshape in the sign; she recognized the full linguistic message of the GIVE₂-*concede* sign to mean that the man wanted to end the discussion. She was not ready to let that happen. This *give* frame took on the form of a discourse marker, guiding the interlocutors during their communicative interaction.

Lexicalization and Grammaticalization of GIVE

Grammatical morphemes retain traces of their earlier meanings even as they acquire different grammatical properties (Bybee and Pagliuca 1994, 46). When GIVE₂-*concede* is used as a discourse marker, as in the discussion above, the morphemes that make up the sign still retain the meanings of their previous forms: (1) The handshape still shows a sense of an "object" through the verb stem that evolved from the LSF classifier sign for coin; (2) the change of control inherent in the prototype sign is still realized; (3) agreement is marked even with the location shift from first person–center to first person–off center; (4) the eye gaze and head tilt, while negative, indicates default contact. Yet the sign no longer means "transfer of control of an object from one person to another." The sign is on its way to a process known in cognitive linguistics as grammaticalization.

In understanding the origins of language change, the study of grammaticalization has become useful to cognitive linguists. Traditionally, this has meant studying the historical changes of a lexical item in its unidirectional path toward becoming a grammatical item. For example, grammaticalization of the English word *will* spans a documented period of approximately one thousand years and results in a semantic change from meaning "want" to meaning "future" (Bybee et al. 1994, 24). Traditionally, lexicalization is the process of linguistic material becoming a lexical item. English lexical morphemes can have such rich specific meanings that their uses are narrow—for example, *stroll, saunter, swim, slide.* Grammaticalization, on the other hand, focuses on the diachronic process in the transition between the lexical and grammatical status of morphemes. English words such as *go* and *come* lack specifics and are appropriate for a wider range of contexts (Bybee et al. 1994, 5) Most recently, the line between grammatical and lexical processes has become blurred (Ramat and Hopper 1998). Nevertheless, there are commonly accepted cross-linguistic patterns that operate on words in all spoken languages that result in semantic and grammatical changes.

ASL, in its short two-hundred-year life, does not have the evolutionary history of a language such as English. However, linguistic analysis of ASL *give* constructions sheds light on a possible grammaticalization path in ASL. Grammaticalization paths are frequently similar across spoken languages, thus an understanding of grammaticalization in general can led to a deeper understanding of the lexical and grammatical changes that operate on the everyday language use of ASL.

"As the function of a grammaticalized element narrows, so does the variety of forms" (Thompson and Mulac 1991, 320). This mechanism of change is found to operate on GIVE$_2$-*concede*. With most GIVE signs, flexibility is allowed as to whether one or two hands are used without affecting the change of meaning. In some giving contexts, the use of two hands can indicate more formality, or a greater degree of ceremony, or even a greater quantity of an item being given. Meaning does not drastically change with the use of two hands—usually only the degree is affected. However, with GIVE$_2$-*concede*, there is almost always a restriction to one hand during its execution. It is generally ungrammatical to use a two-handed GIVE$_2$-*concede*.[5] Substituting the verb stem with the GIVE$_1$ prototype handshape also renders the sign to be ungrammatical.

Frequency of use also motivates grammaticalization. Because the act of giving in ASL is basic, the sign occurs extensively. An increase in frequency allows language change to take place more rapidly than if the sign was infrequently used. The meanings, after

---

5. A similar *langue des signes quebecoise* (LSQ) form for "conceding an argument" uses two hands executed from above both shoulders and should not be confused with the one-hand ASL GIVE$_2$-*concede*.

repeated use, end up in contexts where they are subject to new semantic forces. Newman (1996, 277) notes that the phrase *give me* in English is subject to phonological simplification to *gimme*. He notes that the phrases *love me* and *leave me* are not similarly reduced and suggests that this difference is related to frequency of the occurrence of the phrase *give me*. A similar process can be found in the ASL GIMME variant. There is a phonological reduction that parallels the shift in meaning. With its smaller, repeated wrist motions (of agreement), and lack of location movement, GIMME has more of an imperative-request sense ["oh-come-on-give-it-to-me-right-now"], than the conventional meaning of an actual "change of control over an object."

Another aspect of grammaticalization is called subjectification. The original concrete reference to literal *giving* changes and becomes increasingly abstract due to the speaker's involvement. In GIVE₂-*concede* this pragmatic strengthening occurs when the interlocutor determines the direction of the conversation and makes a firm decision to end it by using the discourse marker GIVE₂-*concede*.

Tracking the ASL sign GIVE and its variants reveals a coherent path of lexicalization: (1) a noun representing an old French coin; (2) related LSF verbs, adjectives, and nouns having to do with money exchange; (3) ASL giving constructions of classifiers and frozen conventionalization; (4) ASL signs having to do with permanent possession, money, and value; (5) metaphorical extensions of literal giving verbs; (6) a regional offshoot adjective variant with its underlying sense of money (CROOK); and finally (7) the wholly metaphorical GIVE₂-*concede*. This path of lexicalization provides evi-

Table 3. Lexicalization/Grammaticalization Cline of GIVE in ASL

Noun	Verb	Noun	Discourse Marker
LSF DONNER	GIVE₁ (literal, then metaphorical) GIVE₁-*completive*		
LSF classifier (money-related signs)	GIVE₂ (rotate wrist) GIVE₂-*formally*	CROOK (regional variant)	GIVE₂-*concede*

dence of potential grammaticalization of GIVE in ASL (see table 3).

This analysis of GIVE$_2$-*concede* indicates that semantic extension has taken place and operates on ASL GIVE signs. Functional layering of GIVE morphemes is emerging, with the older forms being retained. The original LSF classifier nouns representing the shape of a coin have extended into verb stems in both LSF and ASL, and have diachronically evolved into GIVE$_2$ in ASL. Both the X-forms and the handle forms of the *giving* frame currently coexist in ASL. The handle form has not necessarily been discarded, but has become frozen into the prototypical *giving* frame. GIVE$_2$-*concede* shows a semantic divergence from GIVE$_2$. The verb stem phonology of both signs has a common etymology but diverges functionally: GIVE$_2$ remains an inflected verb of both literal and metaphorical nature; GIVE$_2$-*concede* has become a verb of metaphorical mapping only, while functioning as a discourse marker in its operations.

Diachronic study allows the possibility of tracing the interaction of different meaning sources and determines how signed words retain remnants of their source meanings while acquiring new semantic mappings. The semantic envelope of GIVE$_2$ is complex. The history of this verb stem is rich with semantic extensions and internal complexity. The cognitive use of this sign is metaphorically and metonymically structured from the external source domains of everyday experience.

Analyzing the *giving* frame in ASL reveals clearly that slight handshape, location, and motion changes can affect the meaning of ASL signs. This study indicates that there is still much to be researched about GIVE, especially in the areas of meaning that underlie arc movements between arguments, hand-spread extensions, and wrist rotations. Two mechanisms of change exhibited in ASL GIVE signs—metaphorical and metonymic extension—reveal successive semantic changes that show ASL is following a process of grammatical evolution that spoken languages follow. Typical grammaticalization paths of many languages reveal that language dealing with concrete physical objects will shift to closer internal subjectivity, then to totally inner subjectivity—exactly what is found with

ASL GIVE signs. Further cross-linguistic study between LSF and ASL diachronic relationships should reveal additional semantic information about the visual gestural languages.

This chapter only touches the surface of the complexity of the *giving* frame in ASL. Obviously, however, many of the semantic extensions that can occur in spoken languages can also occur in ASL. How deaf people typically conceptualize the nonphysical in terms of the physical can help us to examine the intriguing area of metaphorical and metonymic mapping found in all human minds and human languages.

7

TWO DOGS AND A METAPHORICAL CHAIN

Two dogs and a chain. They snarl and bite, yank their heads, jerk and twist their bodies in the dust. Nothing breaks that chain. The dogs are bound together and nothing can free them—except a cultural metaphor.

Language is shaped by human cognition, and there are powerful connections between language and culture. It is impossible to consider the cultural awareness of the American Deaf community without relating to deaf people's common experiences in using their gestural/visual language. Even the simple act of greeting and introducing oneself is different between the users of ASL and the users of spoken English. For example,

> when an English speaking person grasps the hand of a deaf person in an attempt to initiate a greeting common within the hearing society (handshake), this social gesture automatically cuts off the deaf person's ability to respond in ASL. His language articulator (hand) is held in bondage. People who use ASL become aware of the visual and gestural mores and taboos that differ from those found in everyday spoken language experience. It is only natural to suspect that a language modality can stimulate change in linguistic behaviors as well. (Wilcox 1993, 49).

The view of metaphor subscribed to in this book structures abstract domains by means of mappings from concrete domains (Lakoff and Johnson 1980, 1999). The domain of body parts is one such structured concrete domain. The study of metaphors that refer to parts of the body and their functioning contributes to a clearer understanding of how physical experience is projected onto linguistic action (Pauwels 1995, 35).

The ASL poem "The Dogs," created by deaf poet Ella Mae Lentz, contains certain basic metaphorical structures that are found in many languages (e.g., **social relations are spatial relations, social relationship is physical closeness, social constraint is physical constraint**).[1] An intertropic analysis of this poem reveals persuasive evidence of deep psychological structures that exist at the abstract level of linguistic cognitive processing. The use of spatial metaphors and metonyms in ASL—with their visual instantiations and cultural interpretations—produces creative tropic interaction within the linguistic structure of the poem. In the poem the bodies of the two fighting dogs offer rich metonymic and metaphorical intertropic cognitive processing of ASL as it is used by a native signer. The poem also provides us with a cultural view of the various languages that are used by different deaf people within the Deaf community.

The way we interact with other objects, whether animate or inanimate, structures our conceptual system and our language. In turn, our language is influenced by our cultural differences. The physical interaction we humans experience when we encounter an object in our environment can be a source of cultural conceptualization and linguistic difference. Johnson says that in order to survive as organisms, "we must interact with our environment. All such causal interaction requires the exertion of *force*, either as we act upon other objects, or as we are acted upon by them" (1987, 42). Preconceptual gestalts for *force* have worked their way into our system of meaning and the structure of our communications because the experience of force is something basic to all humans. Johnson recognizes that we tend to take for granted how much of our everyday experience is related to our bodies interacting with other objects (42–43). He notes that force is always experienced through interaction, and our experience of force usually involves a single

---

1. "The Dogs," in *The Treasure: Poems by Ella Mae Lentz*. Berkeley: InMotion Press, 1995.

path of motion with varying degrees of power or intensity. Forces have origins, and a sequence of causality is involved. In "The Dogs," the interaction between the two scrapping dogs is vivid. The power struggle between the two animals leads to a deep cultural understanding revealed by the metaphorical and metonymic instantiations found in the prose. Through the physical struggle, language emerges with rich intertropic extensions.

Synopsis of "The Dogs"

The story begins with two dogs eyeing each other, snapping and snarling. One is a proud Doberman with a shiny coat, exquisitely clipped ears, and an absolutely rigid demeanor. He is the ultimate prototype of a smart, well-fed purebred. He uses impeccable English to communicate. The second dog, a mutt, has floppy ears flung over his glaring eyes. He's an uneducated backyard dog, with a rough coat and a macho, in-your-face attitude. He uses the vernacular of the streets. They glare at each another after circling around and around. As much as they hate one other, they can't escape because they are held together by a long metal chain. After lurching and biting, tearing off fur with teeth and nails, they sit facing one another, both breathing hard and fast. Nothing can break those chains—they are bound together for good.

Finally, the Doberman responds, "We may be irrevocably linked together, but I certainly don't care to associate with a low-life animal like yourself!"

The mutt snarls back, "You big-headed, sophisticated snob! I'd like to kill you! And I would 'cept for this chain around my neck. Phooey, I'd be stuck dragging your stinking dead body everywhere I go—damn."

The Doberman reflects for a moment, then rejoins, "Yes, damn the chain."

The mutt asks, "What the hell is this thing for anyway?"

The Doberman again questions why they are chained together. The mutt looks into the eyes of the Doberman, for the first time without hatred and anger, and replies, "It's a link we're stuck with." The Doberman agrees, "It's a bondage we must accept."

Slowly the two dogs realize that this linkage lasts forever, and only if they work in harmony can they become free—metaphorically released from the chain.

Metaphors, Metonyms, and Their Instantiations

Some of the instantiations of metaphorical mappings found in the analysis of "The Dogs" are listed below.[2] The main metaphors in this poem are THE MIND IS A BODY and SOCIAL RELATIONS ARE SPATIAL RELATIONS. Some of the metaphors highlight the class distinctions between the two dogs. Several will be detailed in order to expose the metonymic and metaphorical mappings that take place. The instantiations chosen for extended analysis were selected because they lend understanding to the cultural phenomena revealed later in this chapter.

- THE MIND IS A BODY
- SOCIAL RELATIONS ARE SPATIAL RELATIONS
- Social identity = physical closeness or co-location
- Social unit = physical unity, connectedness
- Social constraint = physical constraint
- Involuntary social unity = involuntary physical connectedness
- Negative social unit = negative physical unit
- Shared social identity = common chain between two dogs
- Social limitations = inability to move
- Ability to achieve social goals = ability to move to a goal in space
- Inability of Deaf community groups to achieve alone = dogs' inability to move alone
- Ability of Deaf community to achieve by cooperation = dogs' ability to move to some other destination together

---

2. An original analysis of "The Dogs" was made with Eve Sweetser, professor at the University of California, Berkeley, during the 1995 Linguistics Institute held at the University of New Mexico in Albuquerque. I am indebted to her work for the current analysis.

- Educated, English-using Deaf community = Doberman
- Less-educated, ASL-using Deaf community = mutt
- Social unity imposed by state of being deaf = chain

In the story told in the poem, the mind is considered to be a body relating to other bodies in space, not a body with internal parts relating to each other. The target domain is social relations, not psychological or intellectual internal workings. The internal structure of the body is a metaphor for the internal structure of the psyche and intellect; the interaction of bodies in space is a metaphor for the social interaction of abstract "selves" (our minds and psyches).

Mapping one source domain onto an abstract target domain by means of metaphor is a central process in the act of conceptualization. But metaphor alone cannot structure mental conception. Metonymy is also crucial to the process. One variant of the metonymic concept allows systematic conceptualization of one thing by means of its relation to another—the part represents the whole. One concept can stand for another. Metonymy, like metaphor, can be conventionalized and used automatically without conscious awareness. An easily perceived part of one thing is used to represent and evoke the whole object.

A basic metonym is produced when the poet outlines the ears of a dog. From those pointed peaks, the whole image schema of a purebred Doberman can be immediately evoked in the minds of native ASL users. This is a classic representation of the part-whole relationship conceived by metonymy, or more specifically, synecdoche, a subtype of metonymy. Next, the poet uses a modified CL:5 (Bent 5 handshape) to represent the flopped-over ears of the mutt; this too creates a mental conceptualization through synecdoche. Producing the ears alone creates a mental conceptualization of the backyard dog.

Another example of synecdoche occurs when the sign CHAIN is produced. The poet first makes the sign for a long chain that links the dogs, establishing the line of bondage that secures the two animals together. Thereafter in the poem she will use a conventional strategy in ASL for indicating quantity greater than three—she will sign only three links of the entire chain. Yet this abbreviated part (three links) represents the whole chain—synecdoche in a traditional form.

A chain is a common physical object found in our everyday world. At its introduction in the poem the chain seems to represent only a simple metonym. But the intertropic play of metaphors and metonyms is complex. The chain, in an intertropic extension, becomes a metaphor with deep cross-cultural revelations. This process is explained later.

Throughout the poem, instantiations that relate to the SOCIAL RELATIONS ARE SPATIAL RELATIONS metaphor are revealed. SOCIAL RELATIONS ARE SPATIAL RELATIONS is easily conceived because our bodies interact with their surrounding territories. People sit next to one another in a restaurant, stand beside each other's bodies on a bus, interact as objects passing one another in the hall, being careful not to bump shoulders. This daily physical interaction of spatial relations helps us to comprehend the more abstract ideas behind SOCIAL RELATIONS ARE SPATIAL RELATIONS. Three instantiations from the SOCIAL RELATIONS ARE SPATIAL RELATIONS metaphor are examined in the following section.

SOCIAL CONSTRAINT = PHYSICAL CONSTRAINT

Social constraint is an abstract social phenomenon. One scene in the poem vividly demonstrates that abstraction and clearly defines a frustrating human condition. The poet shows how the two dogs are tightly chained together. The graphic image of two dogs jerking hard at the chain evokes the physical experience that people might have if bound to a location by someone holding their necks tightly or pulling at their arms or elbows, preventing them from moving.

This physical image of restriction maps onto a social restriction in society that many deaf people are currently experiencing when trying to advance in the academic world. During the last part of the twentieth century, a number of deaf people enrolled in local colleges and universities only to face substantial obstacles in comprehending spoken and written English. Subsequently, many dropped out without graduating. However, since the early 1970s, a ground-swell of laws and policies encouraging educational advancement for deaf people has swept the nation. One of the resources included in this push for advancement is the provision of signed language interpreting services. In 1990, the Americans with Disabilities Act became the latest national act to stipulate the provision of interpreters on a widespread basis. Many deaf people are now established in colleges and universities, succeeding in their quest to obtain degrees or to advance into tenured positions in academia.

On the one hand, society has encouraged educational advancement of deaf people through the use of interpreting services. Deaf professors are now familiar on college campuses. Many choose to use interpreters even if they lipread or speak well. They want to accurately understand what is happening around them at meetings, lectures, seminars, and impromptu sessions with colleagues in the hallways. Deaf scholars are as responsible as their hearing colleagues to "publish or perish," to obtain research grants, and to maintain contacts with other professionals. However, deaf people who use interpreters find that there are still a multitude of barriers preventing them from gaining ready access to communication. This can affect their advancement in academia.

The barriers to obtaining an interpreter are numerous. The interpreting referral office at the university may be small and inadequate, with limited times available for fulfilling a request. The pay scale might be lower than the one offered in the local community, thereby resulting in skillful interpreters accepting jobs off campus. There may not be enough interpreters knowledgeable and capable of interpreting in the varied areas of academic interest: architecture, biology, journalism, linguistics, philosophy, etc. Deaf professors have the same dreams for professional advancement as their hearing counterparts. Yet, before they can enter a lecture hall or a faculty meeting, they often have to spend an inordinate amount of time figuring out how to obtain the services of a good interpreter.

Enlightened universities are beginning to provide appropriate interpreters to some of their deaf professors who have obtained tenure or tenure-track status. One solution has been to provide specialist interpreters who also serve as research assistants. However, many deaf professors must still contact the university's local referral office in advance, check to verify that their request is being processed, make certain that the appropriate interpreter is available, and so on. Some professors have to suffer the indignity of obtaining "permission" to use an interpreter from an administrator each time they begin the arduous request process. There are often limited interpreting funds. Tough choices have to be made—which meeting or colloquium is most critical to attend? Which one must the deaf person sit out due to limited funding? The unending search for adequate interpreting services is time-consuming and frustrating.

When the poet offers the mental image of a restraint around a dog's neck, it is easy to evoke the image of a deaf person trying to free himself from educational constraints. Deaf professors strain daily for professional excellence while simultaneously fighting barriers that prevent them from achieving it. Hearing professors simply get up, shut their office doors, and walk to a meeting. The deaf professor may have begun planning weeks earlier in order to have adequate interpreting service for the same meeting. Society's constraint—requiring excellence while preventing access—is vividly displayed in the dog's struggle against the chain. The imposition that prevents advancement due to inadequate interpreting services is exemplified in the metaphorical instantiation SOCIAL CONSTRAINT = PHYSICAL CONSTRAINT (see fig. 41).

Figure 41. Social constraint = Physical constraint

INVOLUNTARY SOCIAL UNITY = INVOLUNTARY PHYSICAL
CONNECTEDNESS

The poet creates a *complex metonym* in this instantiation. Two fists
are held up in the signing space in front of the body. With wrists
facing each other, the fists represent the heads of the two dogs facing one other. The wrists metonymically represent the necks and
bodies of the dogs fighting. Facing each other, the fists are yanked
apart, stopping violently as though bound and chained to one
other (see fig. 42). Due to the invisible, metonymically evoked
chain linking them, the fists can only be yanked a few inches apart.
The force is tremendous, however, and brings forth the image of
two individuals facing each other involuntarily, coping with
tremendous rage as they try to break away, knowing full well as
they glare into each other's eyes that they are doomed to an endless
physical connection.

Involuntary social unity is something that deaf and hard of hearing people frequently experience. Although not as graphic as the
poet's rendition, a common source of frustration is found within
events in the Deaf community. One example occurs in the artistic
milieu. Across America, more production companies are now
opening their theaters to deaf audiences by hiring sign language interpreters to be centered near or on the stage. Vision is essential to
all deaf people who want to enjoy theatrical productions. In cities
with large deaf populations, such as Washington, D.C.; Austin,
Texas; and Rochester, New York, plays are often presented with a

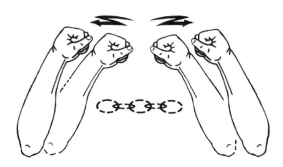

Figure 42. Involuntary social unity = Involuntary physical connectedness

full cast of deaf actors or other accommodations (real-time captioning, FM systems, etc.) that make theatergoing a pleasure. However, smaller Deaf communities often have to attend cultural events where perhaps only a pair of interpreters are provided.

Typical hearing patrons enter the theater and sit where they wish, limited only by the price of their tickets. Deaf people, on the other hand, are usually seated together due to their dependency on vision. Being close to the action on stage is essential and allows deaf and hard of hearing theatergoers to see the signed dialogue or lipread the actors. In the front rows typically reserved for deaf audiences can be found a multitude of diverse groups that make up the "Deaf community." There may be radical ASL users who refuse to even look at another deaf person who chooses to use spoken language—speech—for communication purposes. Sitting next to them might be a man who decided to undergo a cochlear implant in hopes of recovering remnants of his hearing. Down the row might be an oral deaf woman who wishes to lipread in an attempt to blend into society at large. Several other deaf people might prefer to use a form of signed English, which places ASL words in the syntactic word order of English, resulting in a bastardized form of ASL. A couple of young people might even use a phonetic form of "cued speech" that has no ASL words in its repertoire—a communicative puzzle to every deaf person who has not learned those phonetic hand configurations that flit about the mouth and throat.

These individuals, with their diverse communication styles and cultural values, will all be guided to the front rows of the theater for an evening of entertainment. Whereas deaf groups with different communicative preferences usually find ways to distance themselves during other aspects of their social lives, at a theater where vision is the number one channel toward understanding, the groups are often seated together. The visual need that brings deaf groups together serves as an involuntary physical connectedness. The poet's two fists, facing each other, yanking violently apart but being forced to remain in close physical contact, is a visual metaphor for the *involuntary social unity* that occasionally occurs in the Deaf community.

The hearing world at large may be unaware of the radically different communication preferences and the antagonistic feelings that some deaf people have toward one another. Like the theater owners who hire the interpreters and reserve seats for the deaf population in the front rows, the general public believes that "reasonable accommodations" have been provided. Yet sitting in the darkness of the theater, in *involuntary social unity*, may be many deaf and hard of hearing people herded together to the front rows only because of their shared need for light.

NEGATIVE SOCIAL UNIT = NEGATIVE PHYSICAL UNIT

NEGATIVE SOCIAL UNIT = NEGATIVE PHYSICAL UNIT is a metaphoric and metonymic interplay enacted by the poet when she consecutively assumes the personalities of the two dogs. First the Doberman is shown to act like a haughty snob. Then the mutt begins shooting off at the mouth, showing his disdain for the bigger animal. At one point the mutt yells that he wants to kill the Doberman. He is full of anger at the pretentious animal that is so much bigger than himself. He pauses in thought—if he actually killed the other dog, it would fall to the ground as a dead weight. That dead body would become a physical burden tied to the mutt's own neck. Yes, he would be free to walk around at will, but this heavy animal would be dragging behind him every step of the way—pulling on his body, on his neck, on his head. The poet graphically shows how the dead dog would become a physical extension of the mutt.

This *negative physical unit* that the poet so vividly demonstrates maps onto the target domain in NEGATIVE SOCIAL UNIT = NEGATIVE PHYSICAL UNIT. Society in general has little awareness of the animosity that various deaf and hard of hearing groups feel toward one another at times. Deaf and hard of hearing people are sometimes erroneously considered to be a single homogeneous group, called "hearing impaired" by an unenlightened public. The reality is that over the years these groups have developed different cultural values (see fig. 43). Fifty years ago, for the most part, there was a spirit of congeniality among most deaf and hard of hearing people. In the last thirty years, social, legal, and educational changes have created divisions within the deaf population in America. Deaf people who grew up together in state institutions often cherish the memories of their time at the residential schools for the deaf. This is where they learned ASL. Many developed lifelong friendships that are deeper than the bonds they have with their own biological families. They are becoming aware of, and are embracing, a cultural heritage that goes back over two hundred years, to the use of French Sign Language.

At the other end of the spectrum are oral individuals, exemplified by the 1995 Miss America, Heather Whitestone. These individuals expend tremendous amounts of time and energy in their effort to learn to speak the common tongue of the hearing com-

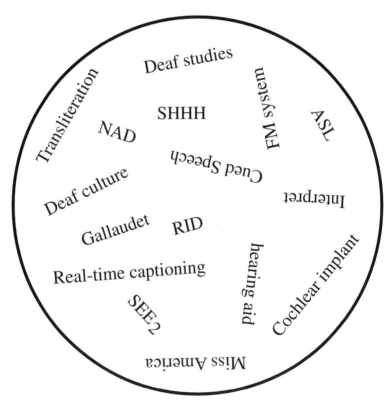

Figure 43. Negative social unit = Negative physical unit

munity. Since ASL does not incorporate speech, and because English is an auditory language, militants in the two deaf groups—one who refuses to honor the language of the oppressor, and the other who daily practices to speak the language—are often on opposite sides of the communication fence. In the middle are a multitude of deaf and hard of hearing people, some of whom may have only recently begun to lose their hearing while others function as bilinguals in society, alternately using ASL and signed or spoken English. Many attended public schools, though in self-contained classes. These classes are considered to be ghettos by the strict oral proponents who believe that putting deaf people together might result in interbreeding that could lead to even more deaf people being born. On the other hand, radical ASL users believe that mainstreaming and inclusion are akin to cultural genocide; they think that deaf children should be in state residential schools for the deaf, not isolated from their deaf peers and fellow ASL users. Hundreds of thousands of other deaf and hard of hearing people are working to find an acceptable middle ground on the diverse communication field.

Government policies and laws have been passed in recent decades to assist deaf individuals in their interaction with American society: the Rehabilitation Act of 1973; the Accessibility in Employment, Education, Health, Welfare, and Social Service Act of 1973; the Education for All Handicapped Children Act of 1975; the Court Interpreter's Act of 1978; the Americans with Disabilities Act of 1990; and the Individuals with Disabilities Education Act of 1990 and 1997. Numerous private and governmental agencies have provided grants for educational, medical, interpreting, research, or mental health programs. These grants sometimes favor one group over the needs or objections of another. They spawn disgruntlement in groups when preferred communication needs are not addressed, and rebellion when the laws force values upon deaf groups that they personally reject.

The different size of the two dogs in the poem is no coincidence. The number of deaf people who use ASL as their primary language make up a small percentage of the total population of deaf and hard of hearing people. Robust demographics are hard to find; the last national census of the deaf population took place in 1974 (Schein and Delk). But estimates place the proportion of people who became deaf or hard of hearing before the age of three—thereby being in a tenable position to learn ASL as a native language—at approximately 14.6 percent. People who became deaf or hard of hearing between the ages of three and eighteen compose 11 percent. The vast majority of deaf and hard of hearing people—72 percent—lost their hearing after the age of eighteen.[3] The smaller mutt has reason to be wary of a huge dead weight. To rebel against a disproportionate number of people who are auditorily identical to themselves encourages social disenchantment. The language scene that deaf and hard of hearing people are born into, or the cultural decision they make to use ASL or not, may be the only thing that distinguishes them from one another. If a small group of deaf consumers demands legislation that benefits themselves exclusively, a substantially larger population of deaf and hard of hearing people may react strongly to these laws. Legislatures pay attention to numbers as well as to issues. Cooperation among all deaf and hard of hearing populations is critical for the cohesive advancement of civil rights for deaf people.

Frank Turk, a lifelong leader in the National Association of the Deaf, has noted a deepening division between deaf people who use ASL and deaf people who also embrace signed or spoken English in their daily lives. He lectures across the country, urging deaf people everywhere to accept the diversity that varied language use can bring into the Deaf community. He urges them to consolidate their political power. Al Couthen, a younger advocate of multilingual and multicultural interaction, is an outspoken leader in the Black Deaf community. He sees the same resistance building up across America and eloquently lectures for the acceptance of diverse language needs as common goals to be achieved by all. These two men look at the widening split within the Deaf community and realize

---

3. Demographics Office, Gallaudet University, Washington, D.C., June 14, 1999.

that the issue of preferred language is beginning to define political goals. They know that the Deaf community will lose its political strength if its number base is splintered. They believe that it is essential for deaf people to regroup if they are to be recognized by state and national legislative bodies.

The metaphor NEGATIVE SOCIAL UNIT = NEGATIVE PHYSICAL UNIT has different facets, but one aspect of reality is that deepening divisions occur when all deaf and hard of hearing people are labeled as a singular unit by society. Stephen Carter, a black law professor, recognizes a similar problem with another minority group in our society and rails against "this societal insistence on rendering complexity simple, on squeezing people into preformed boxes" (1991, 2). The ultimate goal may be to work together harmoniously, but falsely grouping all deaf people into one unit—"one size fits all"— without recognizing and respecting their dissimilarities will not meet the needs of this distinct population.

In the three instantiations discussed above, the poet has created a blend of metaphors and metonyms that demonstrate vividly the cognitive power of human thought processes. *Social relations* in society are mapped from the physical force of the dogs' struggle for release. The *physical constraint* of a chain is equated with the frustrating *social constraint* faced by deaf people living and working in a world controlled by hearing people. *Involuntary social unity* can be created by society but often breeds discontent when the *physical connectedness* is not voluntary or self-motivated. The *negative social unit* that society stamps on diverse deaf and hard of hearing groups can lead to anger if their diversity is not recognized and respected.

In the next section the poet deftly shows how the dogs are eventually released from their state of combat with the chain. Metaphor and metonym intertwine to create a word that shows the power of the mind to transcend physical restraints. The polytropic word that the poet creates is simultaneously metonymic in relation to the whole object (the chain) and metaphoric in relation to the process (being released).

ASL has a conventional sign that means "to let go of something." It can be glossed into English as RELEASE. The index fingers and thumbs link together then pop open to indicate releasing hold of something. This sign can be used to show a literal joining together of two objects, such as links on a chain, and a subsequent releasing of the links. The citation form has a definite detachment gesture at the end, with the fingers and thumbs ceasing to touch one another and ending a few inches apart (see fig. 44a). However, the poet's *RELEASE is an unconventional sign that is not seen in standard ASL usage (see fig. 44b). It is, nevertheless, a brilliant use of metaphor to express the deep meaning in the final creative image. The poet blends *RELEASE into the final word in the poem, FREEDOM. Instead of popping open the fingers in the form of a latch opening, the poet shows that the dogs are "released" from the chain's bondage without opening her fingers and thumb; the fingers glide over each other without a conventional release. The metonymy of the chain represents the part-whole continuity within the entire semantic domain.

This lack of perceptual motion—the absence of a releasing gesture—is a subtle phonological movement that adds profound meaning to her poem. The poet's use of "poetic license" on this unconventionalized *RELEASE shows that the dogs have not truly been released from their bondage. Just like the unconventionalized sign itself, they are destined to remain linked together—and linked to their deafness—forever. The freedom shown here takes on an almost Zen-like quality. The dogs accept their differences and begin to work together as one, accepting their chain of deafness. Freedom comes not from the release of physical bondage but from the acceptance of bondage (or deafness). Accepting who they are and who others are does not change the reality of the bondage, but it does free them metaphorically.

The poet's creativity strikes to the core of what it means to be deaf. Regardless of their differences and of their determination to move freely in respect for those differences, deafness binds them irrevocably.

TWO DOGS AND A METAPHORICAL CHAIN

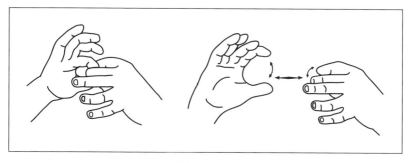

(a) RELEASE

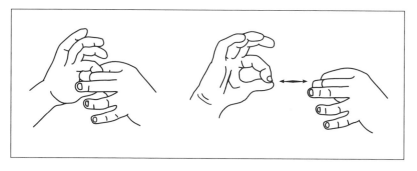

(b) *RELEASE

Figure 44. Conventional and unconventional RELEASE

Cultural Impact on Metaphorical Mapping

Culture can impact language production and word formation through metaphorical conceptualization. Metaphorical expressions typically capture understanding already found within the daily experiences of the group members of a culture. In turn, different cultural groups may view the same image differently. "Meaning is not determined in any direct way by objective reality—instead it is a matter of how we construe or structure a situation in our cognitive representation of it" (Langacker 1985, 110). Metaphor and metonymy play profound roles in the shared understanding that is realized by the words that deaf people use.

Cross-cultural examination of sign languages shows that culture plays a central role in understanding for deaf people around the world. For example, in Japanese Sign Language (JSL), the area surrounding the belly button and chest is considered to be the center of thought. Signs related to thinking are initiated in that location. This is in contrast to ASL, where active thought process is indicated near the frontal portion of the forehead. There is a difference between the two countries' mental concepts for happiness too. Deaf Americans accept the metaphor HAPPY IS UP. Instantiations of that metaphor produce signed expressions that incorporate an upward movement of the hands. Japanese pleasure and happiness is considered to have a more calming effect upon the body; many of their signs reflect this cultural belief by gently sweeping downward or outward. The JSL sign for HAPPY moves forward and downward from the jaw, and the signs for RICH and PROMOTION project outward, rather than upward. Because the metaphors DOWN IS BAD, SAD IS DOWN, and SICKNESS AND DEATH ARE DOWN are pervasive in ASL, the downward and outward motion pattern could confuse a deaf American unfamiliar with the metaphors found in JSL.

Speakers of a language must be able to comprehend the metaphorical and metonymic representations in the language through cultural experience or the communicators will not have the same image-schema needed to understand each other. According to Schneider, "the world at large, nature, the facts of life, whatever they may be, are always part of man's perception of them as that perception is formulated through his culture. The world at large is not, indeed it cannot be, independent of the way in which his culture formulates his vision of what he is seeing. . . . Reality is itself constructed by the beliefs, understandings, and comprehensions entailed in cultural meanings." (1976, 204). In the poet's example, simple objects such as dogs and a chain create a complex, culturally laden mental construct.

One of the most intriguing aspects of the analysis in this chapter involves the conceptualization of a convoluted metaphor and metonym that was not once signed by the poet. Recall that the

poet showed the graphic image of two dogs tightly chained together, yanking hard at their restraint, evoking the metaphor IN-
VOLUNTARY SOCIAL UNITY = INVOLUNTARY PHYSICAL CONNECTED-
NESS (see fig. 42). Although the poet did make the sign LINK when
producing a chain in previous instances, during this particular
complex metonym she did not make a sign for either LINK or
CHAIN. Her fists and wrists were approximately one foot apart,
palms facing, pulling hard so that the counterforce created an
image of the two dogs' heads yanking apart. This creates a
metonym of both synecdoche (part represents the whole) and
contiguity, where contiguity represents proximity or an associa-
tive relationship between two entities. The dogs' heads (fists) and
necks (wrists) hold up the chain (invisible and unsigned). Consultants commented on the chain at this point, although only the
heads and necks (fists and wrists) were signed by the poet. Nevertheless, there was mental conceptualization of a chain wrapped
around each wrist due to the counterforce of the fists being
pulled apart. The metonym of a chain was conceptualized even
though no physical sign was articulated. Not only was the
metonym conceived, but a powerful metaphor representing constraint and struggle between two entities was mapped also—
again without a sign for the chain being made by the poet. Consultants suggested that this chain (invisible and unsigned) stood
for "deafness" or "struggle with deafness".

One seasoned interpreter's remarks exemplify the various comments made by the American deaf and hearing individuals who
viewed the videotape poem and commented on it immediately af-
terwards: "It's obviously a struggle between deaf people who prefer
or have a habit of using signed English compared to those who use
ASL." This was also the prevailing opinion of the ASL consultants
who viewed the poem. However, careful review revealed that the
poet did not sign the word DEAF once throughout the entire poem.
The fact that consultants would automatically assume a metaphor
of deafness and map it onto the metonym of the invisible chain reveals the power that metaphor and metonymy have in our cognitive
processes.

Recently the signed variants glossed as DEAF have begun to be analyzed for syntactic and semantic context. Lucas (1995) collected data on ASL signed variants of "deaf" in combination with other signs. She found an apparent preference for chin-to-ear or contact-cheek over ear-to-chin in the compounds DEAF-CULTURE and DEAF-WORLD (Lucas 1995, 20).

To test the strength of the metaphor of deafness in "The Dogs," the consultants were asked to identify which variant the poet had used when signing DEAF. This question was asked after the first viewing of the poem because many of the consultants referred to what they considered to be an obvious "struggle with deafness" taking place. Responses were obtained in the form of anecdotes from consultants. Viewers typically *recalled* (author's emphasis) either the ear-to-chin or the chin-to-ear form; occasionally they even offered, "maybe the old sign—the ears-are-closed" (dominant index finger touches ear, then both hands meet in center sign space with the two-hand CL:5). After responding, the consultants watched the videotape a second time to verify how the poet signed DEAF. All were surprised when they realized that no sign for DEAF had been used even once in the entire poem.

This raises the question: What made fluent users of ASL determine that the poet was referring to two *deaf* dogs in the poem? Where did the concept of the "struggle with deafness" come from? The poet did not sign the word *deaf*. The mapping came from a cultural experience rather than from any literal lexeme signed in the poem.

As described throughout this chapter, recent political struggles surrounding cultural issues in the United States are pushing apart groups that used to be harmonious and cohesive. The coherent and easily understood metaphorical instantiations of INVOLUNTARY SOCIAL UNITY = INVOLUNTARY PHYSICAL CONNECTEDNESS and NEGATIVE SOCIAL UNIT = NEGATIVE PHYSICAL UNIT bear this out. Language-use issues in education and politics are creating chasms between groups of deaf and hard of hearing people who only two or three decades ago were bonded strongly together. This movement is slowly insinuating itself into every aspect of life in the United States. Educational programs cannot develop curricula without argument over which language will be used in the classroom. Deaf adults who wish to attend public meetings are now facing tough political choices as to which language their interpreter will use. National association conventions are proposing resolutions with opposite viewpoints on language use for their memberships to vote upon. In many areas, middle ground is shrinking. This dichotomy creates a cultural model of American deaf people at extreme odds with one another over language choice, and this difference of communication maps readily onto the dogs and the chain in the poem.

It is interesting to note the different conceptualizations of this poem made by groups of deaf people from two other countries, Switzerland and Italy. When these European deaf people commented on the poem, disparate mappings took place. During a workshop of approximately thirty Swiss-German deaf scholars, the author was discussing metaphors and metonymy in ASL. (The workshop was conducted in ASL/Swiss-German signed languages with skilled interpreters available). At one point, "The Dogs" was analyzed by the entire group, most of whom were sophisticated in metaphor theory. Since ASL users in the U.S. had readily identified the two dogs as being deaf, the author was discussing this aspect of the mapping. Several Swiss-German deaf people raised their hands in puzzlement. They said that they did not envision two deaf dogs. When asked what the poem meant to them, the Zurich group was in agreement that *one* of the dogs was deaf and the *other* was hearing. In addition, the chain was not seen as a metaphor for deafness; it simply appeared to represent a restraint holding the hearing person and the deaf person together as they struggled against one another.

A few also suggested a second mapping: the dogs represented an extension of the "self," with one dog representing the part of self that felt "hearing" and the other representing the part of self that felt "deaf." Indeed, the poet often talked about her own struggle with the acceptance of ASL as a natural language in society. Many of her earlier poems were signed in English word order. Perhaps the poet saw the two dogs as two parts of her own psyche, much like these Swiss-German scholars. The INVOLUNTARY SOCIAL UNITY = INVOLUNTARY PHYSICAL CONNECTEDNESS metaphor was still conceptually mapped, but none of them felt comfortable having two *deaf* dogs fight against each other. The idea seemed alien to the Swiss-German deaf people analyzing the poem. The cultural value of bonding and supporting one another was so intense among these deaf individuals from Switzerland that they could not accept the idea that two deaf people would have a reason to fight against one another in the intense way displayed by the poem. Thus, the conceptual mapping of "deafness" onto both of the dogs and the chain did not occur to them even when that mapping was presented to them by the author.

The author also visited with a group of Italian deaf individuals at the National Research Council in Rome (Reparto di Neuropsicologia del Linguaggio e Sordità). These researchers were interested in metaphor theory, and so "The Dogs" was again presented for analysis, with the usual verbatim translation and preliminary explanations provided for participants who were not familiar with ASL. Immediately following the viewing of the videotape, the group was asked to discuss the various mappings found in the poem.

This group of Italian deaf sign language researchers did not map a conceptualization of "deafness" onto either dog. In fact, no mapping of deafness took place. Instead the deaf Italians looked at the two dogs and saw two different *races* fighting between themselves. In fact, during the discussion about why there was no conceptualization of deaf dogs in the story, one person appeared to speak for all when she explained, "To be deaf means to be together, and to be stronger." Once again, European deaf people felt such a unifying bond of fellowship toward each other that they could not imagine fighting among themselves like the two dogs were doing. They instead mapped "struggle for freedom" and "fighting for freedom" onto the chain and conceptualized each dog as representing a race, or a country of people, fighting against one another.

While the different mappings were initially surprising to this American author, they should not be. Utterances acquire meanings according to culturally shared models. The two dogs took on the mapping of two races by the Italian deaf people. Wars between nations arc something that many deaf Americans do not personally experience. But Italy has been involved in numerous military conflicts during the past century. The recent carnage in Croatia, Bosnia, and Kosovo took place directly across the sea from their country. The wars that American deaf people consider to be far away are separated by only a small body of water from Italian deaf people. That experiential frame of reference provided a different mental conceptualization of the fighting dogs.

Metaphors and metonyms capture existing understandings that people have about their own cultures. Different frames of reference by three separate deaf cultural groups—Americans, Swiss-German, and Italians—created mappings that differed according to their daily experiences. The dogs in the poem were seen as two deaf dogs; a hearing dog and a deaf dog; deaf self and hearing self; or two different races or countries. The chain was alternately mapped as deafness; struggle with deafness; a simple restraining chain; or a struggle or fight for national freedom. The analysis of the mappings of the simple poem viewed by different cultural groups has revealed how cultures influence the way deaf people interpret poems and language.

This chapter reflects the human ability to conceptualize aspects of cultural experiences into language. The embodiment of language and poetry, whether at the phonological, word, phrase, or cultural level affects our conceptual system. Poets often use a variety of strategies to overcome what they see as an estrangement exerted by language between words we use and our bodily experiences (Berntsen 1999, 111). Berntsen wonders what the effect would be "if only the body could become concretely incorporated with the writing and if only the written words could concretely penetrate the body" (113). In ASL the deaf poet and her signed words meld into one. Metonymic mapping is embodied by the poet representing the "part," and the poem, with all its metaphorical and intertropic abstractions, representing the "whole." A metonymic contiguity of both the physical and the abstract is achieved.

Who knows what modality and cultural impacts will be found when linguists begin to seriously study the metaphorical mappings of both spoken and signed languages. Indeed, Fauconnier (1997) alludes to other complex cognitive activities that are not restricted to humans, deaf or hearing. He suggests that other biological animals, mammals in particular, engage in elaborate social and cultural cognitive mappings (1997, 190). The evolution of language, with its metaphorical and tropic processes, may not be restricted to humans. The "metaphors we live by" are waiting for linguists of both signed and spoken languages to begin the analysis.

References

Aitchison, J. 1987. *Words in the mind: An introduction to the mental lexicon.* New York: Basil Blackwell.

Armstrong, D. 1983. Iconicity, arbitrariness, and duality of patterning in signed and spoken languages: Perspectives on language evolution. *Sign Language Studies* 38:51–69.

Baker, C., and D. Cokely. 1980. *American Sign Language: A teacher's resource text on grammar and culture.* Silver Spring, Md.: T.J. Publishers.

Basso, K. H. 1976. "Wise Words" of the Western Apache: Metaphor and semantic theory. In *Meaning in anthropology,* ed. K. Basso and H. A. Selby. Albuquerque: University of New Mexico Press.

Battison, R. 1978. *Lexical borrowing in American Sign Language.* Silver Spring, Md.: Linkstok Press.

Beardsley, M. C. 1976. Metaphor and falsity. *Journal of Aesthetics and Art Criticism* 35:218–22.

Berntsen, D. 1999. How is modernist poetry "embodied"? *Metaphor and Symbol* 14 (2):101–22.

Black, M. 1962. Metaphor. In *Models and metaphors,* ed. M. Black. Ithaca, N.Y.: Cornell University Press.

Boas, F. 1943. Recent anthropology. *Science* 98 (311–14):334–37.

Bolinger, D. 1985. The inherent iconism of intonation. In *Iconicity in syntax,* ed. J. Haiman. Amsterdam: John Benjamins.

Boyes-Braem, P. 1981. Features of the handshape in American Sign Language. Ph.D. diss., Department of Linguistics, University of California, Berkeley.

Brennan, M. 1990. Word formation in British Sign Language. Ph.D. diss., University of Stockholm.

Brugman, C. 1990. What is the invariance hypothesis? *Cognitive Linguistics* 1 (2):257–66.

Bybee, J. L. 1985. Diagrammatic iconicity in stem-inflection relations. In *Iconicity in syntax,* ed. J. Haiman. Amsterdam: John Benjamins.

Bybee, J., R. Perkins, and W. Pagliuca. 1994. *The evolution of grammar: Tense, aspect, and modality in the languages of the world.* Chicago: University of Chicago Press.

196

REFERENCES

Carter, S. L. 1991. *Reflections of an affirmative action baby*. New York: Basic Books.

Chiappe, D. L. 1998. Similarity, relevance, and the comparison process. *Metaphor and Symbol* 13 (1):17–30.

Cienki, A. 1998. STRAIGHT: An image schema and its metaphorical extensions. *Cognitive Linguistics* 9 (2):107–49.

Croft, W. 1990. *Typology and universals*. Cambridge: Cambridge University Press.

———. 1991. Metaphor, metonymy and the conceptual unity of domain. Paper read at Second International Cognitive Linguistics Conference, at Santa Cruz, Calif.

Crystal, D. 1987. *The Cambridge encyclopedia of language*. Cambridge: Cambridge University Press.

D'Andrade, R. 1987. A folk model of the mind. In *Cultural models in language and thought*, ed. D. Holland and N. Q. Holland. New York: Cambridge University Press.

Davidson, D. 1981. *Inquiries into truth and interpretation*. Oxford: Clarendon Press.

DeMatteo, A. 1977. Visual imagery and visual analogues. In *On the other hand: New perspectives on American Sign Language*, ed. L. Friedman. New York: Academic Press.

Diren, R., and R. Langacker. 1990. Call for contributions for Cognitive Linguistics Research. *Cognitive Linguistics* 2:179.

Durham, D., and J. Fernandez. 1991. Tropical dominions: The figurative struggle over domains of belonging and apartness in Africa. In *Beyond metaphor: The theory of tropes in anthropology*, ed. J. Fernandez. Stanford: Stanford University Press.

Eastman, G. 1993. *Epic on the Gallaudet Revolution*. Burtonsville, Md.: Sign Media. Videotape.

Emmorey, K., and S. Casey. 1995. A comparison of spatial language in English and American Sign Language. *Sign Language Studies* 88:255–88.

Fauconnier, G. 1985. *Mental spaces*. Cambridge, Mass.: MIT Press.

———. 1997. *Mappings in thought and language*. New York: Cambridge University Press.

Fauconnier, G., and E. Sweetser. 1996. *Spaces, worlds, and grammar*. Chicago: University of Chicago Press.

Fernandez, J. W. 1986. *Persuasions and performances: The play of tropes in culture*. Bloomington: Indiana University Press.

Fetterman, D. M. 1989. *Ethnography: Step by step*. Newbury Park, Calif.: Sage Publications.

REFERENCES

Fillmore, C., ed. 1982. *Towards a descriptive framework for spatial deixis.* London: John Wiley.

Fischer, S. D. 1980. The issue of variation: Some consequences for sign language research methodology. In *First international symposium on sign language research,* ed. I. Ahlgren and B. Bergman. Stockholm: Swedish National Association of the Deaf.

Fishman, P. M. 1983. Interaction: The work women do. In *Language: Social psychological perspectives,* ed. B. Thorne, C. Kramarae, and N. Henley. Cambridge, Mass.: Newbury House.

Fleischman, S. 1989. Temporal distance: A basic linguistic metaphor. *Studies in Language* 13 (1):1–50.

Friedman, L. A., ed. 1977. *On the other hand: New perspectives on American Sign Language.* New York: Academic Press.

Friedrich, P. 1991. Polytropy. In *Beyond metaphor: The theory of tropes in anthropology,* ed. J. Fernandez. Stanford: Stanford University Press.

Frishberg, N. 1975. Arbitrariness and iconicity: Historical change in American Sign Language. *Language* 51:676–710.

———. 1976. Some aspects of the historical development of signs in American Sign Language. Ph.D. diss., University of California, San Diego.

Frishberg, N., and B. Gough. 1973. Morphology in American Sign Language. La Jolla, Calif.: Salk Institute for Biological Studies.

Gee, J. P., and J. A. Kegl. 1982. Semantic perspicuity and the locative hypothesis: Implications for acquisition. *Journal of Education* 3:185–209.

Gibb, H., and R. Wales. 1990. Metaphor or simile: Psychological determinants of the differential use of each sentence form. *Metaphor and Symbolic Activity* 5 (4):199–213.

Girod, M. 1997a. *La langue des signes: Dictionnaire bilingue LSF/français.* Vincennes: International Visual Theatre.

———. 1997b. *La langue des signes: Tome 3. Dictionnaire bilingue LSF/français.* Vincennes: International Visual Theatre.

Givón, T. 1985. Iconicity, isomorphism and non-arbitrary coding in syntax. In *Iconicity in syntax,* ed. J. Haiman. Amsterdam: John Benjamins.

———. 1991. Isomorphism in the grammatical code: Cognitive and biological considerations. *Studies in Language* 15 (1):85–114.

Goossens, L. 1990. Metaphtonymy: The interaction of metaphor and metonymy in expressions for linguistic action. *Cognitive Linguistics* 1 (3):323–40.

Gregory, M. E., and N. L. Mergler. 1990. Metaphor comprehension: In search of literal truth, possible sense, and metaphoricity. *Metaphor and Symbolic Activity* 5 (3):151–73.

REFERENCES

Gregory, R. L., ed. 1987. *The Oxford companion to the mind*. New York: Oxford University Press.

Groode, J. L. 1992. *Fingerspelling, Expressive and Receptive Fluency*. San Diego: DawnSignPress. Videotape.

Haiman, J. 1980. Dictionaries and encyclopedias. *Lingua* 50:329–57.

———, ed. 1985. *Iconicity in syntax*. Amsterdam: John Benjamins.

Halliday, M. 1985. *An introduction to functional grammar*. London: Edward Arnold.

Hawking, S. 1988. *A brief history of time: From the big bang to black holes*. New York: Bantam Books.

Higgins, D. D. 1923. *How to talk to the deaf*. St. Louis: D. D. Higgins.

Hopper, P., and E. Traugott. 1993. *Grammaticalization*. New York: Cambridge University Press.

Jakel, O. 1993. The metaphorical concept of mind: Mental activity is manipulation. *L.A.U.D. Series A: General and Theoretical Papers* 333:1–25.

Janzen, T. 1995. A description of PUT, a dependent classifier, and an aspectual marker in ASL. University of New Mexico. Typescript.

———. 1998. Topicality in ASL: Information ordering, constituent structure, and the function of topic marking. Ph.D. diss., Dept. of Linguistics, University of New Mexico, Albuquerque.

Johnson, M. 1987. *The body in the mind: The bodily basis of meaning, imagination, and reason*. Chicago: University of Chicago Press.

John-Steiner, V. 1985. *Notebooks of the mind*. Albuquerque: University of New Mexico Press.

Kittay, E. 1987. *Metaphor: Its cognitive force and linguistic structure*. New York: Oxford University Press.

Klima, E., and U. Bellugi. 1979. *The signs of language*. Cambridge, Mass.: Harvard University Press.

Kövecses, Z. 1991. Happiness: A definitional effort. *Metaphor and Symbolic Activity* 6:29–46.

Lakoff, G. 1986. A figure of thought. *Metaphor and Symbolic Activity* 1 (3):215–25.

———. 1987a. Image metaphors. *Metaphor and Symbolic Activity* 2 (3):219–22.

———. 1987b. *Women, fire, and dangerous things: What categories reveal about the mind*. Chicago: University of Chicago Press.

———. 1990. The invariance hypotheses: Is abstract reason based on image-schemas? *Cognitive Linguistics* 1 (1):39–74.

Lakoff, G., and M. Johnson. 1980. *Metaphors we live by*. Chicago: University of Chicago Press.

REFERENCES

———. 1999. *Philosophy in the flesh: The embodied mind and its challenge to Western thought*. New York: Basic Books.

Lakoff, G., and M. Turner. 1989. *More than cool reason: A field guide to poetic metaphor*. Chicago: University of Chicago Press.

Lambert, P. M. L. 1865. *La Langage: De La Physionomie et Du Geste*. Paris: Jacques 6 Lecoffre, Libraire-Editeur.

Lane, H. 1984. *When the mind hears: A history of the deaf*. New York: Random House.

Lane, H., R. Hoffmeister, and B. Bahan. 1996. *A journey into the Deaf-world*. San Diego: DawnSignPress.

Langacker, R. W. 1985. Observations and speculations on subjectivity. In *Iconicity in Syntax*, ed. J. Haiman. Amsterdam: John Benjamins.

———. 1986. An introduction to cognitive grammar. *Cognitive Science* 10:1–40.

———. 1988. An overview of cognitive grammar. *Current Issues of Cognitive Theory* 50:3–49.

———. 1990. Subjectification. *Cognitive Linguistics* 1:5–38.

———. 1991. *Foundations of cognitive grammar*. Vol. 2. Stanford: Stanford University Press.

Lentz, E. M. 1995. *The Treasure*: InMotion Press. Videotape.

Lévi-Strauss, C. 1967. *Structural anthropology*. New York: Doubleday.

Liddell, S. K. 1990. Four functions of a locus: Reexamining the structure of space in ASL. In *Sign language research: Theoretical issues*, ed. C. Lucas. Washington, D.C.: Gallaudet University Press.

———. 1998. Grounded blends, gestures, and conceptual shifts. *Cognitive Linguistics* 9 (3):283–314.

Lindner, S. 1981. A lexico-semantic analysis of verb-particle constructions with up and out. Ph.D. diss., University of California, San Diego.

Long, J. S. 1918. *The sign language: A manual of signs, illustrated, being a descriptive vocabulary of signs used by the deaf of the United States and Canada*. Omaha: D. L. Thompson.

Lucas, C. 1995. Sociolinguistic variation in ASL: The case of DEAF. In *Sociolinguistics in Deaf communities*, ed. C. Lucas. Washington, D.C.: Gallaudet University Press.

———, ed. 1989. *The sociolinguistics of the Deaf community*. San Diego: Academic Press.

Lucas, C., and C. Valli. 1989. Language contact in the American Deaf community. In *The sociolinguistics of the Deaf community*, ed. C. Lucas. San Diego: Academic Press.

Mac Cormac, E. R. 1985. *A cognitive theory of metaphor*. Cambridge, Mass.: MIT Press.

REFERENCES

Mandel, M. A. 1977. Iconic devices in American Sign Language. In *On the other hand: New perspectives on American Sign Language,* ed. L. A. Friedman. New York: Academic Press.

McDonald, B. H. 1982. Aspects of the American Sign Language predicate system. Ph.D. diss., University of Buffalo.

McIntire, M. 1977. The acquisition of American Sign Language hand configurations. *Sign Language Studies* 16:247–66.

Michaels, J. W. 1923. *A handbook of the sign language of the deaf.* Atlanta: Home Mission Board, Southern Baptist Convention.

Moody, B. 1986a. *La Langue des signes: Tome 2. Dictionnaire bilingue elementaire.* Vincennes: International Visual Theatre.

———. 1986b. *La Langue des signes: Tome 3. Dictionnaire bilingue elementaire.* Vincennes: International Visual Theatre.

Mow, S. 1989. How do you dance without music? In *American Deaf culture: An anthology,* ed. S. Wilcox. Silver Spring, Md.: Linstok Press.

Moy, A. 1990. A psycholinguistic approach to categorizing handshapes in American Sign Language: Is [A$_s$] an allophone of /A/? In *Sign language research: Theoretical issues,* ed. C. Lucas. Washington, D.C.: Gallaudet University Press.

Newkirk, D. 1987. *Architech: Final version (Signfont handbook).* San Diego: Emerson and Stern Associates.

Newman, J. 1994. GIVE: A cognitive linguistic study. New Zealand: Massey University.

———. 1996. *Give: A Cognitive Linguistic Study.* Berlin: Mouton de Gruyter.

———, ed. 1998. *The linguistics of giving.* Amsterdam: John Benjamins.

Norwell, E. 1989. Conversation features and gender in ASL. In *The sociolinguistics of the Deaf community,* ed. C. Lucas. San Diego: Academic Press.

O'Brien, J. 1999. Metaphoricity in the signs of American Sign Language. *Metaphor and Symbol* 143:159–77.

Ohnuki-Tierney, E. 1991. Embedding and transforming polytrope: The monkey as self in Japanese culture. In *Beyond metaphor: The theory of tropes in anthropology,* ed. J. Fernandez. Stanford: Stanford University Press.

Padden, C. 1980. The Deaf community and the culture of Deaf people. In *Sign language and the Deaf community,* ed. C. Baker and R. Battison. Silver Spring, Md.: National Association of the Deaf.

Padden, C., and T. Humphries. 1988. *Deaf in America: Voices from a culture.* Cambridge, Mass.: Harvard University Press.

REFERENCES

Paivio, A., J. C. Yuille, and B. A. Madigan. 1968. Concreteness, imagery and meaningfulness values for 925 nouns. *Journal of Experimental Psychology* 76 (1, pt. 2):1–25.

Patrie, C. J. 1997. *Fingerspelled names and introductions*. San Diego: Dawn-SignPress. Videotape.

Pauwels, P. 1995. Levels of metaphorization: The case of put. In *By word of mouth: Metaphor, metonmy and linguistic action in a cognitive perspective*, ed. J. L. Mey, H. Parret, and J. Verschueren. Amsterdam: John Benjamins.

Pesmen, D. 1991. Reasonable and unreasonable worlds: Some expectations of coherence in culture implied by the prohibition of mixed metaphor. In *Beyond metaphor: The theory of tropes in anthropology*, ed. J. W. Fernandez. Stanford: Stanford University Press.

Quinn, A. 1982. *Figures of speech: 60 ways to turn a phrase*. Salt Lake City: Gibbs. M. Smith.

Ramat, A., and P. Hopper, eds. 1998. *The limits of grammaticalization*. Amsterdam: John Benjamins.

Reddy, M. 1979. The conduit metaphor—a case of frame conflict in our language about language. In *Metaphor and thought*, ed. A. Ortony. Cambridge: Cambridge University Press.

Rice, S. 1998. Giving and taking in Chipewyan: The semantics of THING-marking classificatory verbs. In *The linguistics of giving*, ed. J. Newman. Amsterdam: John Benjamins.

Richards, I. A. 1936. *The philosophy of rhetoric*. Oxford: Oxford University Press.

Rosch, E. 1973. Natural categories. *Cognitive Psychology* 4:328–50.

Rosch, E., and B. Lloyd, eds. 1978. *Cognition and categorization*. Hillsdale, N.J.: Lawrence Erlbaum Associates.

Rutherford, S. D. 1988. The culture of American Deaf people. *Sign Language Studies* 59:129–47.

———. 1989. Funny in Deaf—not in hearing. In *American Deaf culture: An anthology*, ed. S. Wilcox. Silver Spring, Md.: Linstok Press.

Schein, J. D., and M. T. Delk. 1974. *The Deaf population of the United States*. Silver Spring, Md.: National Association of the Deaf.

Schneider, D. M. 1976. Notes toward a theory of culture. In *Meaning in anthropology*, ed. K. Basso and H. Selby. Albuquerque: University of New Mexico Press.

Searle, J. 1979. *Expression and meaning: Studies in the theory of speech acts*. New York: Cambridge University Press.

Spradley, J. P. 1979. *The ethnographic interview*. New York: Holt, Rinehart and Winston.

REFERENCES

Stokoe, W. C. 1978. *Sign language structure*. Buffalo: University of Buffalo Dept. of Anthropology and Linguistics, 1960. Reprint, Silver Spring, Md.: Linstok Press.

———. 1990. An historical perspective on sign language research: A personal view. In *Sign language research: Theoretical issues*, ed. C. Lucas. Washington, D.C.: Gallaudet University Press.

Stokoe, W. C., D. Casterline, and C. Croneberg. 1976. *A dictionary of American Sign Language on linguistic principles*. Washington, D.C.: Gallaudet College Press, 1965. Reprint, Silver Spring, Md.: Linstok Press.

Supalla, T. 1978. Morphology of verbs of motion and location in American Sign Language. In *Second national symposium on sign language research and teaching*, ed. F. Caccamise. Silver Spring, Md.: National Association of the Deaf.

Supalla, T., and E. L. Newport. 1978. How many seats in a chair? In *Understanding language through sign language research*, ed. P. Siple. New York: Academic Press.

Sutton, V. 1981. *Sign writing for everyday use*. Newport Beach, Calif.: Center for Sutton Movement Writing.

Svorou, S. 1986. On the evolutionary paths of locative expressions. In *Berkeley Linguistic Society*, ed. K. Nikiforidou, M. Vanclay, M. Niepokiy and D. Feder. Berkeley: Berkeley Linguistic Society.

Sweetser, E. 1987a. The definition of LIE. In *Cultural models in language and thought*, ed. D. Holland and N. Quinn. Cambridge: Cambridge University Press.

———. 1987b. Metaphorical models of thought and speech: A comparison of historical directions and metaphorical mappings in the two domains. In *Proceedings of the thirteenth annual meeting of the Berkeley linguistic society*, ed. J. Aske, N. Beery and L. Michaelis. Berkeley: University of California, Berkeley.

———. 1990. *From etymology to pragmatics: Metaphorical and cultural aspects of semantic structure*. Cambridge: Cambridge University Press.

———. 1992a. English metaphors for language: Motivations, conventions, and creativity. *Poetics Today* (Winter):705–24.

———. 1992b. "Inside/outside, upside down"—Co-orientation of metaphorical mappings in literary and everyday language. Paper read at UCLA's Clark Library Conference, at University of California, Berkeley.

Talmy, L. 1983. How language structures space. In *Spatial orientation: Theory, research, and application*, ed. H. Peck and L. Acredolo. New York: Plenum Press.

Taub, S. Forthcoming. *Language in the body: Iconicity and conceptual metaphor in American Sign Language*. Cambridge: Cambridge University Press.

203

REFERNCES

Thompson, S., and A. Mulac. 1991. A quantitative perspective on the grammaticalization of epistemic parentheticals in English. In *Approaches to Grammaticalization*, ed. E. C. Traugott and B. Heine. Amsterdam: John Benjamins.

Traugott, E. C. 1974. Explorations in linguistic elaboration; language change, language acquisition, and the genesis of spatio-temporal terms. In *Historical linguistics*, ed. J. M. Anderson and C. Jones. Amsterdam: North Holland.

———. 1982. From propositional to textual and expressive meanings: Some semantic-pragmatic aspects of grammaticalization. In *Perspectives on historical linguistics*, ed. W. P. Lehmann and Y. Malkiel. Amsterdam: John Benjamins.

———. 1985. Conditional markers. In *Iconicity in syntax*, ed. J. Haiman. Amsterdam: John Benjamins.

Traugott, E., and E. Konig. 1991. The semantics-pragmatics of grammaticalization revisited. In *Approaches to grammaticalization*, ed. E. C. Traugott and B. Heine. Amsterdam: John Benjamins.

Trick, L., and A. T. Katz. 1986. The domain interaction approach to metaphor processing: Relating individual differences and metaphor characteristics. *Metaphor and Symbolic Activities* 1 (3):185–213.

Turner, M. 1990. Aspects of the invariance hypothesis. *Cognitive Linguistics* 1:247–55.

———. 1991. *Reading minds: The study of English in the age of cognitive science*. Princeton, N.J.: Princeton University Press.

Turner, T. 1991. "We are parrots," "Twins are birds": Play of tropes as operational structure. In *Beyond metaphor: The theory of tropes in anthropology*, ed. J. W. Fernandez. Stanford: Stanford University Press.

Valli, C. 1990. *Poetry in motion*. Burtonsville, Md.: Sign Media. Videotape.

Valli, C., and C. Lucas. 1995. *Linguistics of American Sign Language: An introduction*. 2d ed. Washington, D.C.: Gallaudet University Press.

van Hoek, K. 1988. Mental space and sign space. Paper read at Linguistics Society of America Conference, at New Orleans, La.

———. 1992. Conceptual spaces and pronominal reference in American Sign Language. *Nordic Journal of Linguistics* 15:183–99.

Wilbur, R. B. 1987. *American Sign Language: Linguistic and applied dimensions*. Boston: College-Hill Press.

Wilcox, P. 1993. Metaphorical mapping in American Sign Language. Ph.D. diss., University of New Mexico, Albuquerque.

———. 1998. GIVE: Acts of giving in American Sign Language. In *The linguistics of giving*, ed. J. Newman. Amsterdam: John Benjamins.

Wilcox, S. 1992. *The phonetics of fingerspelling*. Amsterdam: John Benjamins.

REFERENCES

———, ed. 1989. *American Deaf culture: An anthology*. Silver Spring, Md.: Linstok Press.

Wilcox, S., and P. Wilcox. 1997. *Learning to see: Teaching American Sign Language as a second language*. Washington, D.C.: Gallaudet University Press.

Zadeh, L. 1965. Fuzzy sets. *Information and Control* 8:338–53.

INDEX

INDEX

INDEX